# KNOW YOUR SHAKESPEARE

# KNOW YOUR

# SHAKESPEARE

By John Calvin Metcalf

FORMER LINDEN KENT PROFESSOR OF ENGLISH LITERATURE
THE UNIVERSITY OF VIRGINIA

*Fain would mine eyes be witness with mine ears.*
I Henry VI, ii, 3

D. C. HEATH AND COMPANY BOSTON

# FOREWORD

WHY another book on Shakespeare? Certainly there is nothing essentially new to be said about him; any kind of introduction will necessarily involve considerable repetition of well-known facts and theories. But the manner of approach will doubtless continue to vary from decade to decade. In spite of the multiplicity of books about Shakespeare, he, like all other "classics," needs to be introduced to each generation of readers, for the emphasis shifts from age to age in the interpretation of so complex a genius. He himself, to whom "all the world's a stage," has to be dramatized again and again. The student or general reader may be pardoned for feeling perplexed at the accumulating mass and variety of interpretative material in the numerous "companions" to Shakespeare. In the extensive information about Shakespeare the non-professional reader may find himself, as it were, in a tangled forest of comment and conjecture and may conclude that this Shakespeare is a portentous fellow indeed if an understanding of him requires such formidable accompaniment. It is to simplify the approach to Shakespeare and to light up what he has called "the dark backward and abysm of time" that this brief presentation of Shakespearean characteristics has been prepared, in the hope that it may help to make the reading and study of his plays and poems more rewarding.

I wish to thank my former colleagues, Dean James S. Wilson and Professor Walter A. Montgomery of the University of Virginia, for reading and commenting on my manuscript. I am deeply indebted to Professor Archibald B. Shepperson and Mr. Marvin B. Perry, Jr. of the same university for their active interest in the publication of this book.

*J. C. M.*

# CONTENTS

# KNOW YOUR SHAKESPEARE

# *Know Your Shakespeare*

London in 1616, dominated by old St. Paul's cathedral.
From John Vischer's *View of London*

## THE AGE OF SHAKESPEARE

ELIZABETHAN England was a golden
age in poetry and drama as well as in statecraft and exploration. The nation, politically
strong and commercially prosperous, was also
intellectually productive. After the autocratic
reign of Henry VIII (1509–1547), the short,
ineffectual reign of his son Edward VI, and the

period of religious intolerance under Henry's daughter Mary, Henry's younger daughter Elizabeth won enduring popularity among her subjects and undying fame. Her glamorous personality, her masterful leadership, and her encouragement of genius, whether in politics, discovery, or letters, won for her the enthusiastic loyalty of Englishmen and the envy of other nations. Her many faults were like sunspots which, by contrast, make the rest of the luminary more bright; or, to use a favorite Elizabethan figure, her faults were mere foils to her virtues. In her actions and accomplishments the Queen was the embodiment of her age, "the observed of all observers, the rose and expectancy of the fair state."

The most signal national triumph of her long reign was the victory over the Spanish Armada in 1588, which made England supreme on the sea. It was the beginning of that primacy in sea power which her writers have celebrated in song and story ever since. Above all, this and subsequent victories united the English people in patriotic devotion to their Queen and inspired in them an invincible optimism. In the play *Richard II*, which is about the king who reigned two hundred years before Elizabeth, Shakespeare makes old John of Gaunt utter

Queen Elizabeth attired for the royal thanksgiving on the
defeat of the Armada

a famous speech which must have won from audiences in Elizabethan theatres a hearty response, for in most memories the victory over Spain was still fresh:

> This royal throne of kings, this sceptered isle,
> This earth of majesty, this seat of Mars,
> This other Eden, this demi-Paradise,
> This fortress built by Nature for herself
> Against the infection and the hand of war,
> This happy breed of men, this little world,
> This precious stone set in the silver sea,
> Which serves it in the office of a wall,
> Or as a moat defensive to a house,
> Against the envy of less happier lands;
> This blessed plot, this earth, this realm, this
>                         England.

The Elizabethan Age was an era of creative vigor that revealed itself most notably in the production of plays which are remarkable both for variety and quality. They reflect in a marked degree the democratic tendencies in literature. Hitherto literature in general had been aristocratic, following classical models. But the newer poetry and prose was less imitative, with a definite appeal to popular taste; the middle-class citizen and even the peasant began to appear as characters in the drama of the day. In the play of *Hamlet*, written about 1600, the Prince of Denmark says to his friend Horatio, after a flippant reply by the gravedigger to the Prince's questions: "By the Lord, Horatio, these three years I have taken note of it; the age is grown so picked [choice] that the toe of the peasant comes so near the heel of the courtier he galls his kibe [chilblain]." That is, the upper classes are now hard pressed by the lower. Now, this popularizing of literature, particularly of the drama, not only afforded playwrights like Shakespeare an opportunity to express themselves freely, but it made theatre-going a favorite recreation as well as an educational medium for the masses.

Long before Shakespeare's day, however, the English drama had entertained and instructed the people in the form of religious, moral, and other plays. These, known collectively as the Mystery and Miracle plays, dealing with Bible stories, the Moralities, teaching moral lessons, folk plays on popular heroes and traditions, and short farces (interludes), were presented in various towns. The four great cycles of the Mystery plays, given out of doors, lasted far into the Elizabethan Age, as did the Moralities also; and out of the interludes or farces grew comedy. School plays, such as

*Gammer Gurton's Needle* and *Ralph Roister Doister*, and other adaptations of classical models, tragedies like *Gorboduc*, imitating Latin plays and intended for cultured audiences, were other pre-Shakespearean dramas. All these varieties, as well as translations of contemporary Italian plays, Shakespeare may have seen in his youth, for even the Miracle and Morality plays were occasionally presented in Elizabeth's reign as survivals of popular forms, allusions to which are found in Shakespeare's own plays. As far as poetic drama is concerned, however, it was Shakespeare's early contemporary, Christopher Marlowe, who showed by the range and splendor of his imagination and the magnificence of his verse the capabilities of poetry as a medium of dramatic expression.

London was, of course, the center of the varied activities of the great age of Shakespeare. The English capital still had somewhat the appearance of a mediaeval city, with its walls, narrow streets, and closely built houses, its shop-lined bridge across the Thames, and its famous Tower, believed to have been built, in part at least, by Julius Caesar. In this rather quaint capital city was the royal court at Whitehall, along the banks of the Thames were the city houses of the great nobles, and in the heart of the city were many churches. Here also were the law courts and the Royal Exchange, financial center of the kingdom, and numerous taverns. Across the river, along the bankside, were most of the theatres. The one building of sixteenth-century London toward which all movement tended was St. Paul's Cathedral, the old church which was burned in the great fire of 1666. It was both a religious sanctuary and a social center, the gathering-place of men of all professions who met their friends and clients in the spacious nave. For the poets and dramatists, however, a favorite resort was the clublike Mermaid Tavern near St. Paul's. In a verse-letter to Ben Jonson, literary dictator of the day, his fellow poet and playwright Francis Beaumont paid tribute to that popular rendezvous:

> What things have we seen
> Done at the Mermaid! heard words that have been
> So nimble and so full of subtle flame,
> As if that every one from whence they came
> Had meant to put his whole wit in jest
> And had resolved to live a fool the rest
> Of his dull life! . . . And when we were gone,
> We left an air behind us, which alone
> Was able to make the two next companies
> Right witty! though but downright fools, more
> wise!

The England of Shakespeare, as reflected in its verse and prose and above all in its vast and varied drama, was in the main a merry England, with an insatiable zest for living. The Elizabethan entered into his sports and other pleasures with a dashing abandon, often with a riotous prodigality and recklessness which we attribute to young giants at their play in some heroic age of fable. He loved rich dress, showy spectacles, gay tournaments, the glitter and pomp of royal processions. Elizabethan life was full of excesses and sharp contrasts, of clashes between poverty and wealth, of the startling proximity of squalor and splendor. This red-blooded buoyancy, this youthful joyousness, physically relieved itself in fencing, boxing, wrestling and other manly sports, in bear-baiting and cock-fighting; and intellectually, in writing sonnets or essays or in composing and acting plays. Aesthetically, the Elizabethan found satisfaction in music, in song and dance, and in his poetic "praise of ladies dead and lovely knights." In him there was a strange blending of the pagan and the Christian which was true of the Renaissance in general.

Shakespeare came when the English Renaissance was at high tide and all the currents of national life were running strong. The shadow of a growing Puritanism had not yet fallen athwart the land and dulled the joy of living. Cakes and ale were still plentiful in old England and ginger was still hot in the mouth. Falstaff and Sir Toby were unashamed reprobates dear to the distracted multitude. In the heyday of this period of supreme dramatic creation William Shakespeare had found his inspiration, working with materials which the London scene afforded and giving contemporary coloring to the rich inheritance of past ages. Then almost suddenly, perhaps sensing the coming change, he forsook the city of his creative years and went back to his home town. And that little town on the Avon still celebrates the Man of Stratford with festivals of song and dance and the annual production of his plays.

John Shakespeare's house in Stratford-upon-Avon as it
looked in the eighteenth century

## THE MAN FROM STRATFORD

THOSE Elizabethans who, as we think,
most deserved biographies either had none
or, at best, only sketchy stories of their lives.
Numerous "lives" of Queen Elizabeth have
been written in the last hundred years, based on
official documents, letters, contemporary references, and imagination. This has also been true
of her great courtiers and ministers of state,
men like Leicester, Essex, and Raleigh. Raleigh
had an adventurous life, suffered years of im-
prisonment, and was beheaded under Elizabeth's successor. But he wrote his *History of*

*the World,* partly a spiritual autobiography, which has helped to immortalize him. We know a good deal about Francis Bacon because he was an eminent political figure, a great lawyer and philosopher with a scientific spirit, who wrote learned works on statecraft, classical tradition, and essays on the practical conduct of life. Socially, he was an aristocrat. Moreover, dismissal from his high judicial office gave him considerable notoriety. These men of high estate spoke and wrote "for the record," as we say today, and so had their activities publicized. It was different with the poets and dramatists, men often obscure socially, poor, and dependent for prestige, and even for a livelihood, upon the uncertain favor of princes and lords. Literature was not a profession but an avocation wherein genius was sometimes praised but too often starved. The greatest Elizabethan non-dramatic poet, Edmund Spenser, has had no complete biography. With him, as with most of his literary contemporaries, we try to find the man in what he wrote. What we lack in recorded fact we seek to discover in his work.

How far Shakespeare portrayed himself in his works is a question almost as futile as it is fascinating. Matthew Arnold implies such "foiled searching" in his sonnet to Shakespeare:

Others abide our question. Thou art free.
We ask and ask: Thou smilest and art still,
Out-topping knowledge. For the loftiest hill
That to the stars uncrowns his majesty,
Planting his steadfast footsteps in the sea,
Making the heaven of Heavens his dwelling-place,
Spares but the cloudy border of his base
To the foiled searching of mortality:
And thou who didst the stars and sunbeams know,
Self-schooled, self-scanned, self-honoured, self-
                    secure,
Didst walk on earth unguessed at. Better so!
All pains the immortal spirit must endure,
    All weakness that impairs, all griefs that bow,
    Find their sole voice in that victorious brow.


It is obviously perilous to make a personal ap-
plication of the speeches of a great dramatist.
No doubt a practical playwright and actor like
Shakespeare sometimes speaks through his characters — for there are speeches in the plays so in
accord with certain known facts of his life as
not to be ignored — but, in general, one must
be wary of personal interpretation. Still, when
the factual record fails, as it very often does,
and when we are reduced to excessive use of
"perhaps," "probably," and "possibly," there
is nothing else to do but fall back upon some
suggestive lines. When, for instance, we read

the recommendation in *Twelfth Night* that a woman marry a man older than herself, it is hard not to conclude that Shakespeare is thinking of his own marriage to an older woman. Of course he may simply have been stating a common notion and practice; but why go out of his way to deliver a little lecture? The frequent use in the plays of stage terms like "cue," "omen," "prologue," and the like, reveals the professional knowledge of a regular actor, and so does Hamlet's address to the players. Those last speeches of Prospero in *The Tempest* about actors vanishing like spirits and his decision to "abjure his magic, break his staff, and drown his book," suggest a farewell to the dramatist's art.

Outside the region of conjecture there are, happily, solid stretches of fairly dependable data for the reconstruction of Shakespeare's life. These are, indeed, more numerous than in the lives of many of his poetic and dramatic contemporaries. Of his major fellow dramatists only Ben Jonson has more recorded evidence for the biographer. Jonson was concerned about dramatizing himself to his own and succeeding generations: he published his own works, talked and wrote about himself, boldly expressed his opinions. To a group of young admirers, "the sons of Ben," he was a literary dictator. Shakespeare, on the contrary, had no "sons of Will," and, so far as we know, he took no pains to make sure he would be remembered. We must content ourselves, therefore, by attempting to construct out of scattered material a bridge, so to speak, on a foundation of fact here and there until the highway of his career attains an approach to completeness. Such a process of reconstruction, beginning with the eighteenth century, has resulted in a considerable library of research, the fundamental part of a vaster library of criticism and interpretation.

The materials for a life of Shakespeare consist of contemporary records, or documents, contemporary references and allusions, and later traditions. We know from the register in Trinity Church, Stratford-on-Avon, that William, the son of John Shakespeare, was christened on April 26, 1564. The register in the same church records his burial in the chancel there on April 25, 1616. The inscription on his monument gives April 23 as the day of his death; tradition has it that he died on his birthday. And so April 23, 1564, is the generally accepted date of Shakespeare's birth.

His father, John Shakespeare, was a glover

Trinity Church, where Shakespeare is buried, from
across the Avon River

and dealer in other merchandise who lived and carried on his business in Henley Street. In his prosperous years, before he became involved in debt, he had been alderman and high bailiff, or mayor, of Stratford, then a town of some two thousand people. William Shakespeare's mother was Mary Arden, of a neighboring village, whose family was of a higher social class than her husband's. Of their eight children William was the third, and oldest, son. Of his boyhood little is positively known. That he attended the Stratford Grammar School, where the curriculum was severely classical, seems certain. In his nineteenth year he married Anne Hathaway of Shottery, a village one mile from Stratford. She was a woman seven or eight years his senior. The Hathaway cottage has long been one of the most frequented shrines in the world. Those who have walked to it across the fields from Stratford on a fine early summer day can never forget the charm of the region. Tradition has invested the spot with an atmosphere so enchanting that no one, even though he be unpoetic in temperament, may wholly escape the romantic spell of this scene of a great poet's courtship.

What the young man did in the years immediately following his early marriage is not clear. A later tradition, recorded in Aubrey's *Brief Lives* (1681) and attributed to the actor Beeston, is that Shakespeare "had been in his younger years a schoolmaster in the country." And though Ben Jonson said that "he had but little Latin and less Greek," Beeston thought Shakespeare "understood Latin pretty well." The schoolteaching story is plausible, particularly if taken in connection with the talk of the pedagogue in *Love's Labour's Lost* where Shakespeare shows familiarity with the subjects and instruction in Elizabethan schools. His teaching experience would help to explain Shakespeare's evident knowledge of the favorite Latin authors in the English Renaissance, and might also throw light on his choice of Plautus as the source of his early *Comedy of Errors*. Moreover, several years of country schoolteaching before he went up to London would have been an honest means of support for a wife and three children. Traditional also is the deer-stealing episode in Sir Thomas Lucy's Charlecote Park near Stratford, mentioned by the Reverend Richard Davies about the end of the seventeenth century. This story has served to identify Justice Shallow in *Merry Wives of Windsor* with Sir Thomas, Shakespeare's prosecutor for poaching, whom he supposedly makes fun of in the play. The incident is also said to have been the cause of Shakespeare's flight to London. If this be true, Sir Thomas did the young man a real service; but scholars are skeptical about this explanation of his exit from Stratford.

At any rate, to London Shakespeare went in his early twenties either for love of adventure or to hunt a job. Doubtless he wanted to combine the two. There he must have met Christopher Marlowe and other lively young fellows who hung around the theatres in the Shoreditch region. Youths from the provinces with an itch for acting and playmaking naturally gravitated toward the metropolis, which was small enough in those years (having a population of about a hundred and fifty thousand) for men of like mind to get acquainted promptly. There is a tradition that Shakespeare, along with "several other poor boys belonging to the company," held the horses of fashionable playgoers while the performances were going on. From this lowly occupation, he supposedly became acquainted with "people of quality" as well as with theatrical folk and "was taken into a higher and more honorable employment within doors." From the outside to the inside of the playhouse, from assisting at the presentation of plays to the revision and writing of them, are plausible steps in a progress from dramatic apprenticeship to collaboration and independent authorship. And from what we know of other Elizabethan dramatists this practical association with actors and this firsthand acquaintance with the production of plays were common enough in the making of successful playwrights. In these unrecorded years of apprenticeship Shakespeare evidently learned the technique of an art in which he was to attain mastery not through genius alone but also by the toil and sweat of experimentation.

It has been assumed that Shakespeare reached London in 1585, or the following year, leaving his wife and children in Stratford. For the next seven years there is no record of him. What was he doing in these "silent years"? Did he visit Stratford from time to time? When the Spanish Armada was defeated in 1588 and London went wild with rejoicing, was this future singer of the "sceptered isle" among those celebrating England's triumph? Presumably so. Not until 1592 is there any reference to Shakespeare's accomplishments. In that year Robert Greene, poet, dramatist, and pamphleteer, wrote on his deathbed a farewell attack on those fellow playwrights of whom he was apparently jealous.

One of these he called "an upstart crow, beautified with our feathers, that with his Tiger's heart wrapped in a Player's hide supposes he is as well able to bombast out a blank verse as the best of you: and being an absolute *Johannes factotum*, is in his own conceit the only Shakescene in a country." This almost certainly refers to Shakespeare and is, of course, a bit of grudging evidence of his success as a writer of plays. The "Tiger's heart" quotation is a corruption of a line in *Henry VI, Part 3*, Act I, scene 4: "O tiger's heart wrapped in a woman's hide." After Greene's death his printer, Chettle, a minor dramatist, issued what is considered an apology for this attack on Shakespeare. He compliments Shakespeare for his "civil demeanor" and excellence in acting, referring also to persons of social and political importance who held Shakespeare in high esteem for "his uprightness of dealing" and his grace in writing. That he was at this time engaged in literary labors is proved by the publication, in 1593 and 1594 respectively, of his two narrative poems, *Venus and Adonis* and *The Rape of Lucrece*, to each of which he prefixed an elaborate dedication to Henry Wriothesley, Earl of Southampton.

From that time on the name of Shakespeare

frequently appears. In 1594 he was a member of the Lord Chamberlain's Company of Players who performed before the Queen at Greenwich Palace. In 1596 John Shakespeare was granted a coat of arms, presumably through the efforts of his son, which entitled him to be styled "gentleman." In this last decade of the century Shakespeare, influenced by the prevailing lyric craze, wrote his sonnets, which were circulated in manuscript but not published until 1609. In these years his early comedies, tragedies, and histories were produced. Francis Meres, a young London clergyman, published a small volume in 1598 called *Palladis Tamia: Wit's Treasury* in which he mentions a dozen of Shakespeare's plays, already well known, and includes his name in a list of eminent poets and dramatists. Meres speaks of the "mellifluous and honey-tongued Shakespeare" (referring to his two narrative poems and sonnets), and praises him as "the most excellent among the English" in comedy and tragedy. "The Muses," says Meres, "would speak with Shakespeare's fine-filed phrase, if they would speak English."

Besides the rather frequent mention of Shakespeare as author of plays and allusions to his acting, there are several references to his con-

58 cited by Chambers

nection with business matters and to his places of residence in London. Certain assessments for taxes in St. Helen's, Bishopsgate, where various dramatists were living in the mid-nineties of the sixteenth century, include Shakespeare's name. And we know that in 1597 Shakespeare bought New Place, one of the largest dwellings in Stratford, to which he was to return as a prosperous citizen when his London years were over. The next year Richard Quiney, a fellow townsman, wrote to Shakespeare requesting a loan of thirty pounds to pay debts owed by Quiney in London. Two letters to Quiney about getting money from Shakespeare are also in existence; the three letters afford evidence of the dramatist's financial standing.

The discovery in London by Professor C. W. Wallace, an American scholar, of documents bearing on a lawsuit between a man named Mountjoy and his son-in-law Belott, throws light on Shakespeare's place of residence in the first decade of the seventeenth century. Shakespeare, who lodged at Mountjoy's house at the corner of Silver and Monkwell Streets, had helped to bring about the marriage between his landlord's daughter and his apprentice Belott. Some years later, when Mountjoy had failed to pay the promised dowry, the dramatist testified in Belott's suit against his father-in-law. The signature in the dramatist's statement in the case added another authentic autograph to the five already known to exist. As Shakespeare is described in this document as of Stratford-on-Avon, it would seem that he was then (1612) on a visit to London, having taken up his residence in Stratford a year or more previously. There at New Place as a prominent citizen, interested in local affairs, he spent the last four or five years of his life. He must have visited the metropolis occasionally, and he doubtless had visits from Jonson, Drayton, and other friends. In March of 1616 he made his will, which is still preserved. The story, handed down by the Reverend John Ward of Stratford fifty years after the poet's death, that Drayton, Ben Jonson, and Shakespeare "had a merry meeting, and it seems drank too hard, for Shakespeare died of a fever there contracted," may or may not be true. On the wall over his grave in Trinity Church a monument was erected a few years after his death on which is the world-famous bust by Janssen, with an elaborate inscription in Latin and in English testifying to his genius.

Of Shakespeare's three children the oldest was Susannah; the other two, Judith and Hamnet, were twins. Susannah married Dr. John

Hall, a well-known physician of Stratford. According to her epitaph in Trinity Church, Susannah Hall was notable for her ability, piety, and philanthropy. Shakespeare's son Hamnet died when he was eleven or twelve; Judith married Thomas Quiney, "gentleman," of Stratford, not long before her father's death. As Judith's children died young, Susannah's daughter Elizabeth was alone left of the poet's grandchildren. By her second marriage Susannah became Lady Bernard, wife of Sir John Bernard of Abingdon. With her death in 1670 the short line of Shakespeare's direct descendants ended.

On the journeys between Stratford and London in his fruitful years Shakespeare used to stop in Oxford at the tavern kept by his friends John Davenant and his wife. Thus the poet came to be godfather to their child, who later became the distinguished poet and dramatist, Sir William Davenant. When the boy was twelve years old he wrote "An Ode in Remembrance of Master Shakespeare," whom he had no doubt often seen. Of his spiritual sonship to the great dramatist William Davenant proudly boasted on many occasions throughout his life; he was, moreover, not averse to the unsupported tradition that he was the natural son of Shakespeare.

Of the numerous portraits and busts representing Shakespeare only two are authentic — the engraving on the title page of the First Folio of his plays (1623) and the bust over his grave in Trinity Church. The engraving was by Martin Droeshout and the bust by Gheerart Janssen. The Flower Portrait (so called from the name of the first owner) in the Memorial Library at Stratford resembles the First Folio engraving and may have been the original of it. The Ely Palace portrait in the Birth House is believed by some to be of Shakespeare. The oft-produced Chandos portrait (named for the former owner) — the one with the beard, longer hair, and the earrings — has only tradition in its favor as having been painted by the Elizabethan actor Richard Burbage. All the portraits show a noble brow, but the Chandos is more poetic-looking. "He was a handsome, well-shaped man," said seventeenth-century Aubrey.

No handwriting of Shakespeare is known to exist except the six signatures; these are in the older Elizabethan script. Some scholars have thought that three pages of a manuscript play

about Sir Thomas More are by Shakespeare because of the resemblance of the writing to that
in the signatures, but this is doubtful. The fact
is, most Elizabethan dramatists have left no
scrap of their handwriting: it must be remembered that numerous fires in seventeenth-
century London, together with carelessness in
preserving manuscripts, have robbed later generations of their rightful literary heritage.

Among the tributes to Shakespeare during
his lifetime and immediately afterward by other
dramatists, one of the most noteworthy is that
of John Webster, author of two great tragedies, in whose plays there are many Shakespearean echoes. In addition to those echoes, Webster
speaks of "the right happy and copious indus-
try" of Shakespeare, Dekker, and Heywood,
"wishing what I write may be read by their
light; protesting, that, in the strength of my
own judgment, I know them so worthy, that
though I rest silent in my own work, yet to
most of theirs I dare (without flattery) fix that
of Martial: '*non norunt, haec monumenta
mori* (these monuments do not know how to
die)'." Another playwright, Thomas Freeman,
wrote a sonnet to Shakespeare, and still another
poet left some laudatory verses to him. William
Basse, a younger contemporary, thought Shake-

speare should have been buried in Westminster
Abbey with his poetic peers:

> Renowned Spencer, lye a thought more nye
> To learned Chaucer, and rare Beaumont lye
> A little neerer Spenser to make roome
> For Shakespeare in your threefold fowerfold
> Tombe

A little later Ben Jonson was lavish in his praise.

Prefixed to the famous First Folio of the
plays are tributes from several of Shakespeare's
friends, the most distinguished being Jonson,
who was intimately acquainted with the Stratford dramatist. Jonson bears witness to the
faithfulness of the picture on the title page of
the volume, but wisely advises the reader, if he
would really see Shakespeare, "to look not on
his Picture but his Book." In his memorial lines
Jonson, while praising his dead friend, evidently expresses his sincere conviction that
"He was not of an age, but for all time!" Elsewhere Jonson recorded his sense of personal
devotion and admiration: "I loved the man and
do honor his memory, on this side idolatry, as
much as any. He was indeed honest and of an
open and free nature: he had an excellent phan-
tasy, brave notions, and gentle expressions."

Indeed, the general testimony of Shakespeare's contemporaries is that he was wise, witty, and gentle, a companionable man, whose human qualities were as marked as his gifts of mind and spirit.

Macbeth and the three witches. From Holinshed's
*Chronicles of England Scotlande and Irelande*, 1577

## WHAT SHAKESPEARE READ

REFERENCES and allusions in the plays
indicate that Shakespeare must have read
widely. They do not prove that he was a
scholar, learned in the arts and sciences, but
they do show that he had read many books and
that he freely used material from them. Incidents, names, stories in ancient, mediaeval, and
contemporary history and literature appear,
sometimes with little or no change but more
often varied to suit his immediate purpose. That
purpose was the dramatic presentation of life
as he saw and felt it in his own time. In reading
his plays and poems one is impressed by their

contemporary quality as well as by their time-lessness. They reflect the thought and action of that exceedingly vital period in human history, the Elizabethan Age, which drew from a vast classical tradition as well as from a great native storehouse for its literary material. Much of the classical lore came through a romantic medium, particularly the Italian, since Italy, of all countries in the Renaissance, was the most direct inheritor of ancient learning. Translations in the sixteenth century were so common that a reading knowledge of the ancient and modern tongues was hardly necessary for an acquaintance with the most famous foreign classics. Only a few of the Elizabethan dramatists, such as Ben Jonson and George Chapman, were classical scholars; the others, including Shakespeare, got their knowledge of antiquity more or less indirectly.

Shakespeare got his knowledge of ancient literature partly at school, for the grammar schools of his day were severely classical, but mostly from books he read during his years in London. It may be assumed that he studied Lyly's *Latin Grammar* and Aesop's *Fables*. Of these two standard Elizabethan textbooks there are echoes and reminiscences in a dozen or more of his plays. The Latin poet who apparently most impressed Shakespeare was Ovid. Shakespeare's first published poem, *Venus and Adonis*, is a story taken from Ovid, the motto on the title page of which is a quotation in Latin from that poet. The other Latin poet, quite different in content and method from Ovid, who greatly influenced Shakespeare was Seneca, writer of that form of drama known as "the tragedy of blood." Whether Shakespeare read Seneca in the original is not known; a translation of this poet, as indeed of Ovid, was available. It was Seneca's technique which kept alive in the Elizabethan drama the form (the five-act division) and some of the spirit of classical tragedy, and that form had become conventional by the time Shakespeare got under full headway as a playwright. It may be concluded, then, that Shakespeare was somewhat familiar with Latin, but that he largely depended on translations for his knowledge of Latin authors. He was in all probability entirely dependent upon translations for his limited acquaintance with Greek writers.

One work which Shakespeare read and used extensively was Plutarch's *Lives of Illustrious Men*. This famous collection of Roman and Greek biographies, in Sir Christopher North's translation from a French version of the Greek

original, was published in 1579 and became im-
mensely popular. From it the Elizabethans derived much of their knowledge of the most
eminent classical statesmen and warriors. That
Shakespeare knew his Plutarch thoroughly is
evident from his use of that biographer in his
Roman plays. Sometimes he follows Plutarch's
account almost slavishly, incident for incident; and again, he simply changes the prose
of North's translation into verse. There are
stretches of description in the play of *Antony
and Cleopatra*, for instance, which are the same
in Shakespeare as in Plutarch except for the
metrical arrangement. The play of *Coriolanus*
follows its original closely; *Julius Caesar*, most
popular of the Roman plays, while largely Plu-
tarchian in incident, is freer and richer in characterization, more psychological, more like
*Hamlet*.

Plutarch's *Lives* is a great book, not simply a
series of annals or chronicles, and is the finest
body of prose literature that Shakespeare drew
his plots from. The French essayist Montaigne,
whom Shakespeare knew through Florio's
translation, properly estimated the vital quality
of Plutarch when he declared: "They who
write lives by reason that they take more notice
of counsels than events, more of what proceeds

from within doors than of what happens without, are the fittest for my perusal; and therefore, of all others, Plutarch is the man for me."
Shakespeare found Plutarch fittest for his perusal in writing his Roman plays. His indebted-
ness to Plutarch is also shown here and there in
other dramas. References to Julius Caesar,
whom Horatio in *Hamlet* calls "the mightiest
Julius," and to Antony and his Egyptian en-
chantress in the later play of *Cymbeline*, are
further examples of Shakespeare's familiarity
with Plutarch.

Another prose work of great popularity in
Elizabethan England was Raphael Holinshed's
*Chronicles of England, Scotlande, and Irelande*.
Holinshed was a voluminous compiler of British history, liberally mingled with legendary
lore, from the earliest kings down through the
reign of Henry VIII. In this labor he was as-
sisted by other chroniclers. The second edition
of Holinshed, published in 1587, was the one
Shakespeare used. Of this accumulation of fact
and fiction, truth and myth, Holinshed managed to make a readable story: it is indeed
a narrative of considerable vitality, parts of
which are distinctly dramatic. And so when
Shakespeare decided to write a series of plays
on English history (what are technically called

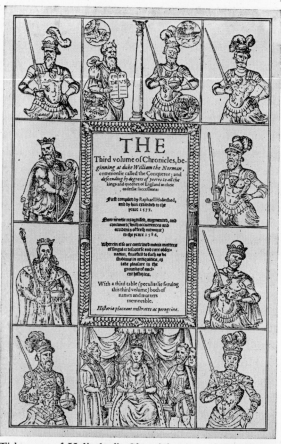

Title page of Holinshed's *Chronicles*, one of the sources
of Shakespeare's plays

"chronicle plays") he naturally turned to Holinshed. The result was the group of dramas on the kings of England from the early thirteenth to the mid-sixteenth century. While all these history plays go under Shakespeare's name, in several of them he was a collaborator rather than sole author. Besides these he wrote others — *Macbeth*, *King Lear*, and *Cymbeline* — in which material from Holinshed was employed. Shakespeare made more use of Holinshed than of any other of his dramatic sources. In composing his British plays he followed Holinshed as he followed Plutarch in his Roman.

Readers of Shakespeare's time had access to numerous collections of old stories on which the playwrights drew freely for their plots. Most of these tales were in Italian and French, but many of them were available in English versions. The Italians called these romantic narratives *novelle* (plural of *novella*). Best known of such collections were Boccaccio's *Decameron*, Bandello's *novelle*, and Cinthio's *Hecatommithi* ("hundred stories"). The last two had been translated into French, and Shakespeare evidently read French, though it has not been proved that he had a reading knowledge of Italian. There was, however, an English translation of some of these romances in the popular collection called *Painter's Palace of Pleasure*. A still larger and more miscellaneous compilation in Latin, *Gesta Romanorum* ("Deeds of the Romans"), furnished materials for Elizabethan storytellers and dramatists. Shakespeare's professional as well as his general reading covered parts of this vast storehouse of ancient and mediaeval fiction. To all this should be added the numerous mediaeval romances in English, including the Arthurian stories, *Guy of Warwick, Bevis of Hampton*, and others, which were well known to the Elizabethans. And there were the English and Scottish ballads and other folklore — books on witchcraft, fairies, and ghosts — with which Shakespeare would naturally have been familiar, as many references in his plays show.

Quite as popular as this older literature was the increasing supply of books and pamphlets on travel. There were collections such as Hakluyt's *Principal Navigations, Voyages and Discoveries*, besides a great number of accounts by contemporary travelers of their marvelous experiences in foreign parts. Among the latter was a pamphlet setting forth the adventures of Sir Thomas Gates, Sir George Sommers, Captain Newport and others, in the shipwreck off the Bermudas of the small fleet headed for Virginia, an account of which Shakespeare made a slight use in *The Tempest*. A book that proved of interest to playwrights and general readers of the day was Eden's *History of Travayle in the West and East Indies*. These are a few examples of an extensive travel literature which an age much given to exploration and adventure found both entertaining and educational.

Some of this popular reading matter, old and new, Shakespeare must have become acquainted with directly, but a good deal of it he doubtless learned through the poets and playwrights of his own country, from Chaucer to Spenser. In Chaucer and Gower, who were mighty story-tellers, he had a rich mine of material. He read the fifteenth-century Caxton's publications of the tales of Troy and Malory's enchanting book on Arthur and his knights; and in his own contemporaries — Spenser, Sidney, Daniel, Drayton, Lodge, Lyly, Greene, and Marlowe — he found matter for some of his plots.

But in an age of supreme dramatic activity, when collaboration and borrowing were common practices, Shakespeare would have become directly acquainted with much of that vast output of plays in London in the last half of the sixteenth century, to say nothing of the earlier

Tudor drama. So great must have been his reading in this rich and varied field that to deal adequately with it would involve a discussion of
the Elizabethan drama as a whole. No doubt his
general reading was considerable, also, and one
is justified in thinking that whatever he read
became grist for his mill. The French dramatist
Molière is reputed to have said, in defense of
his alleged appropriation of the thoughts of
others, "I take my own wherever I find it."
Shakespeare made his own whatever he found
useful in his reading of old chronicles or of old
plays; it is sometimes difficult, indeed, to know
just how much is purely Shakespearean in certain plays.

Included in Shakespeare's general reading
was the Bible. His obvious familiarity with it
justifies the conviction that in childhood he
heard it read in church and school. There were
two English translations of the Scriptures common in his youth, the Geneva Bible and the
Bishops' Bible, one or both of which Shakespeare used. It is true that he wrote no plays on
Biblical subjects, but his references to Biblical
characters and incidents are so frequent as
to imply a thorough acquaintance with their
source. Moreover, he assumes a knowledge of
the Bible on the part of his hearers and readers,

whether he is quoting word for word or less directly. Biblical quotations and allusions in Shakespeare have been identified by scholars and made available to those who need proof that the great dramatist was saturated with a knowledge of that old household English classic which was once and still is an indispensable part of a liberal education.

Shakespeare's reading, it may therefore be concluded, was of two kinds — that which was of a general cultural nature and that which gave him more directly material for his plays. He read those books which were common in the English Renaissance — history, philosophy, poetry, prose fiction. And certainly the two kinds often overlapped; it is impossible to draw any clear line between them. Shakespeare's library would not have been as classical as a scholar's, but more "popular," abounding in contemporary stuff, including pamphlets, romances, folklore, fables, proverbs, travels. He read the standard books and those of the newer ones that appealed to him, for both kinds of reading were necessary for the man whom Ben Jonson characterized as "not of an age, but for all time."

Shakespeare's coat of arms, entitling him to be called "gentleman"

## HOW SHAKESPEARE
### USED HIS READING

IT was from his wide reading in prose fiction, poetry, biography, and chronicles that Shakespeare naturally drew the material for his plays. Thus, most of his comedies are based on old stories from romantic and classical literatures, particularly Italian; the histories on old chronicles, especially Holinshed's popular collection; and the tragedies on similar historical and legendary narratives. Sometimes the dramatist drew directly on the original stories when translations were available, and sometimes on contemporary adaptations of them in verse and prose. Moreover, he revised old plays that were based on material which had proved popular on the stage. There was, for example, an older *Hamlet* which Shakespeare transformed into the great play we know. When you read one of Shakespeare's "sources" and compare it with the Shakespearean play, you are impressed with the vast superiority of his product. You will note that this has been accomplished in the plot by selection, rearrangement, and the addition of new scenes. The ending of the play is often very different from that in the source. But above all, you will observe that the characters in the drama are far more vital and clearcut than those in the story on which Shakespeare drew; indeed, you may make the acquaintance of one or more persons not in the original story. For nowhere does Shakespeare show his genius more strikingly than in the creation of characters. Most of them seem so real that the world accepts them as actual people who loved and laughed and suffered as we do.

Shakespeare's originality, then, is not in the stories he dramatized, for they were known to readers of his time, but in his particular use of

them. He read a crude, wooden narrative of
love or adventure and proceeded to humanize
it and give it artistic form. He read the dry record of an old chronicle and made it come alive.
He often changed the order of events; he also
eliminated that which was unnecessary and
added scenes and characters of his own invention. To the dry bones of a dreary narrative he
gave vitality and made it modern. In doing this
he did not hesitate to change the order of time
by putting in incidents and persons of a later
day. He made the remote and unfamiliar near
and familiar to an Elizabethan audience of men
and women who wanted their history in contemporary terms. And so, like other Renaissance poets and dramatists, Shakespeare gave to
the past the coloring of the present. His characters are, after all, Elizabethan ladies and gentlemen, warriors, heroes, peasants, clowns, villains,
masquerading under different names. We are
not surprised, therefore, to find Shakespeare
"guilty" of numerous anachronisms. If a Greek
or Roman general talks like the Earl of Essex,
and if a Roman rabble acts like an English mob,
we find it perfectly natural. When cannon go
off in the supposedly eleventh-century *Hamlet*
and the clock strikes in *Julius Caesar* and Hec-
tor quotes Aristotle in *Troilus and Cressida* —

well, we accept it as all right, for the cannon and the clock and Aristotelian scholarship were common in Elizabethan England. And ancient warriors, it has already been remarked, wore Elizabethan military dress on the stage. With Shakespeare "the play's the thing" to catch the attention of the audience, and often he succeeds only by violating historical accuracy. You may learn a good deal of English history by reading Shakespeare's kingly plays, but you will also get a good deal of pure fiction in which, like all great dramatists, he tells the truth about human nature.

A comparison of several Shakespearean plays with their main sources will reveal certain typical changes made by the dramatist in the use of them. *Romeo and Juliet* is a simple and definite example of such use. This tale of two lovers, separated by family and fate, who die almost at the moment of reunion, is an old one. In its simplest form the story is traceable to mediaeval Greek romance; passing to Italy, it appeared in an enlarged form among the *novelle* of Bandello. This was followed by Boisteau's French version. In 1562 an English verse translation was made from the French by Arthur Brooke, and on this Shakespeare mainly relied in writing his play. In dramatizing the

Bandello-Brooke story he made five or six
changes, as follows: (1) reduction of the time
from many months in the Brooke poem to four
or five days in the drama; (2) invention of the
quarrel scene at the beginning between the
servants of the two hostile families; (3) introduction of the fiery Tybalt at the Capulet ball;
(4) the re-creation of Mercutio from a poorly
portrayed courtier to a brilliant, witty gentleman; (5) Paris strewing flowers on Juliet's
tomb; (6) the change of Juliet's age from
sixteen to fourteen. Shakespeare's characterization of the nurse is practically an original
creation. But far more important than these im-
provements, Shakespeare gives to the story
movement, clearcut character portrayal, vividness, and lyrical beauty.

In the comedy of *As You Like It* Shakespeare dramatized a popular novel of his own
time, *Rosalynde*, by Thomas Lodge. The play
follows the novel rather closely, but Shakespeare changed the names of some of Lodge's
characters and also, as he generally does, trans-
figured them. Rosalind, for instance, is in
Lodge's novel the conventional maiden of pastoral poetry, talking of tournaments, inspiring
sonnets, extremely beautiful, a highly artificial
creature. Shakespeare's Rosalind is, on the con-

trary, a lively, very real woman with a mind of her own, witty, and ready to give her lover as good as he sends, or better. When Orlando says he will die if she will not have him and cites the fate of well-known rejected lovers, Rosalind replies: "But these are all lies; men have died from time to time and worms have eaten them, but not for love." The following characters in *As You Like It* are Shakespeare's invention: the melancholy Jaques, the court clown Touchstone, Le Beau, William, Audrey, Sir Oliver Martext, and Corin. From the novel come such incidents as the brothers' quarrel, the wrestling match, the escape to the Forest of Arden, the wooing of the disguised Rosalind by Orlando, and the marriage of the elder brother to Celia. The chief changes found in the drama are: (1) the great shortening of the story; (2) the elimination of the warlike elements; (3) the voluntary exile of Celia because of her devotion to her banished cousin Rosalind; and (4) the voluntary abdication of the Duke. The name of the play may have been suggested by a short sentence in the dedication to the novel: "If you like it, so." The speeches in the play are of course Shakespeare's and so are the songs, though a number of lyrics are scattered through the prose tale of Lodge, who was himself a poet.

There are many quotable passages in *As You Like It;* the most famous of these is the "seven ages" soliloquy of Jaques beginning "All the world's a stage," a speech which must have been feelingly composed by the actor-philosopher dramatist. In general, Shakespeare refined and spiritualized Lodge's prose romance by infusing into the action and characters both humor and beauty, and in so doing he wrought out of well-known materials the most charming of pastoral dramas.

*Much Ado about Nothing,* another high comedy of the middle period, is made up of three strands: the Claudio-Hero love story, which is the main plot; the Benedick-Beatrice merry war of words; and the comic distortions of the stupid constable group, which are purely English. These last two strands of the dramatic web are Shakespeare's own invention. The romantic story of the love of Claudio and Hero came to Shakespeare from one of the novels of the Italian Bandello, probably through the French translation of Belforest. He was doubtless also familiar with Ariosto's version of the tale in *Orlando Furioso,* and Spenser's adaptation of it in the *Faerie Queene.* Shakespeare makes one important alteration in the plot. In the old story Claudio denounces Hero to her father and mother through a messenger; she is charged with unfaithfulness to Claudio and the match is broken off. This is a rather tame scene, lacking in dramatic effect. Shakespeare substituted for this the interrupted church wedding (Act IV, scene 1) which is theatrically much more effective, forming as it does the climax of the main plot. Moreover, through the humiliation and supposed death of Hero the major action is linked to the Benedick-Beatrice story, for the latter pair, convinced of Hero's innocence, agree to take vengeance on Claudio. It is characteristic of Shakespeare that his most notable variations from his sources are in the people of his plays rather than in the plots. Take Hero, for instance — the heroine of the play. In Bandello's Hero we have the pale, ineffectual maiden of mediaeval romance. Shakespeare's Hero, on the other hand, is a real woman, sensitive and true. Though she is referred to as the "gentle Hero," she makes a spirited defense and indignantly denies the charge of unfaithfulness. We who read the play wonder how the sensitive and high-toned girl whom Shakespeare created could have forgiven the faithless Claudio. In no other comedy of Shakespeare are the sentimental, the intellectual, and the comic so cleverly interwoven as in the romantic love story, the brilliant combats of wits, and the humorous stupidity which constitute the three strands of this serio-comic play. And at least half of it is Shakespeare's own invention, while practically all the dialogue is his.

One of the great tragedies, *Othello*, will serve to illustrate how Shakespeare used his sources in writing tragedy. He found the story in the *Hundred Tales* of the Italian novelist Giraldi Cinthio. The dramatist follows the main incidents of the novelist except at the end, where he radically departs from the original narrative. In the old story Iago and Othello, after deciding that Desdemona must die for her alleged unfaithfulness, agree on Iago's plan for the murder: Desdemona is to be beaten to death with a stocking filled with sand, and then the ceiling of her chamber is to be pulled down so that a beam may fall on her. Thus the innocent lady is disposed of. But Othello, soon mad with grief, turns upon Iago, degrades him from office and banishes him. In revenge Iago accuses Othello to the captain, who has him arrested, tried, tortured, and banished. Othello is afterwards killed by Desdemona's relatives. Later, Iago, convicted of another murder, is tortured to death; then his wife reveals the circumstances of Desdemona's death. In contrast to this prolonged and bloody conclusion, the swift ending of Shakespeare's drama has a sort of terrible beauty without any physical horror: Desdemona's quiet submission to her fate, foreshadowed in the willow song, Othello's deadly anguish of remorse, and the assurance of speedy torture for the villain complete this pathetic tragedy

> Of one that loved not wisely but too well;
> Of one not easily jealous, but being wrought
> Perplexed in the extreme; of one whose hand,
> Like the base Indian, threw a pearl away
> Richer than all his tribe.

The leading characters in the play, except Desdemona, bear Shakespearean names; all the persons taken over from the old story have been transformed. The refinement, subtlety, and complexity of character are entirely Shakespeare's and, as always, his is the glorious poetry of the dialogue. For crafty insinuation and suggestion the psychological wrestling match between Iago and Othello in the third scene of the third act is unequaled in Elizabethan drama.

The historical plays show fewer variations from their sources than the comedies and tragedies proper, but even in the histories, as already

# The Historie of
## *Henry the Fourth.*

Enter the King, Lord *Iohn* of *Lancaſter*, Earle of
*Weſtmerland*, with others.

### King.

SO ſhaken as we are, ſo wan with care,
    Find we a time for frighted Peace to pant,
    And breath ſhort winded accents of new broiles,
    To be commen'ct in ſtronds a farre remote:
No more the thirſtie entrance of this ſoile,
Shall daube her lips with her owne childrens blood:
No more ſhall trenching Warre chanell her fields,
Nor bruiſe her flowers with the armed hoofes
Of hoſtile paces : thoſe oppoſed eyes,
Which like the Meteors of a troubled heauen,
All of one nature, of one ſubſtance bred,
Did lately meete in the inteſtine ſhocke,
And furious cloſe of ciuill butcherie,
Shall now in mutuall well-beſeeming rankes,
March all one way, and be no more oppoſ'd
Againſt acquaintance, kindred and allyes.
The edge of Warre, like an ill-ſheathed Knife,
No more ſhall cut his Maſter : therefore friends,
As farre as to the Sepulchre of Chriſt,
Whoſe ſouldier now vnder whoſe bleſſed Croſſe
We are impreſſed and ingag'd to fight,
Forthwith a power of *Engliſh* ſhall we leuie,
Whoſe armes were moulded in their mothers wombs,
To chaſe theſe *Pagans* in thoſe holy fields,
Ouer whoſe acres walkt thoſe bleſſed feete,

           Which

The first page of the quarto edition of *Henry IV*,
published in 1598

remarked, Shakespeare invented scenes and added incidents. In *Richard II*, for instance, at least two scenes are Shakespeare's own — the garden scene in the third act and the parting of Richard and his Queen in the fifth act. In the two parts of *Henry IV* a few scenes have been added by the dramatist, and the age of Hotspur has been reduced by twenty or more years to make him a more suitable match in battle with young Prince Hal. But it is in the comic under-plot, centering about Falstaff, that Shakespeare has made his greatest contribution. This he derived not from the chronicle source of the reign of Henry IV but from an old play called *The Famous Victories of Henry the Fifth*, a crude and wooden performance in which Prince Hal and one Sir John Oldcastle figure. Shakespeare put Oldcastle in his first draft of *Henry IV*, but the descendants of that noble gentleman objected to what they considered a degradation of their ancestor's character. Whereupon Shakespeare dropped Sir John Oldcastle and invented Sir John Falstaff, apparently deriving the name, by a transposition of letters, from Sir John Fastolfe, a cowardly character in the first part of *Henry VI*. Two traces of the name Oldcastle were inadvertently carried over in the new play of *Henry IV*: in the first act of Part I the

Prince calls Falstaff "my old lord of the castle";
and in Part II one speech of Falstaff in the first
act is assigned to Oldcastle in the Quarto of
1600. Moreover, in the Epilogue to the second
part of the play it is stated, as if to meet any
possible misunderstanding, that "Oldcastle died
a martyr and this is not the man." The famous
fat knight, Sir John Falstaff, is Shakespeare's
immortal creation. From his entrance on the
stage, through his pranks as boon companion
to Prince Hal, his experience in battle confirm-
ing his philosophy that "the better part of valor
is discretion," his pathetic snubbing by the
prince who had become king, and his final
"babble of green fields" — from first to last he
is supremely human. He is as unforgettable in
the realm of the humorous as Hamlet is in that
of the serious.

These typical illustrations of Shakespeare's
use of his sources in comedy, tragedy, and history make it clear that the dramatist, like all
great creative artists, shows his originality in
the modification of old material and, above all,
in his reconstruction of the characters from
mere lay figures or puppets into beings of flesh
and blood who are true to human nature in any
time or place.

The Globe Theatre ("Shakespeare's theatre"), South-
wark, c. 1612. From Wilkinson's *Theatrum Illustrata*

# HOW THE PLAYS
## REACHED THE PLAYERS

HOW the knowledge gained from reading
and observation was shaped into the product we call a play is the playwright's secret.
Shakespeare, like other Elizabethan dramatists,
did not discuss the theory of the art he prac-
tised with high distinction. Here are the plays:
we may study them and deduce, if we can, certain principles and methods which we may call
the philosophy and technique, the dramaturgy,
of Shakespeare. Thousands of scholars have

tried this fascinating game. But they have not been able to pluck out the heart of the playwright's mystery any more than the readers of *Hamlet* have succeeded in solving the Prince of Denmark's. And this mystery about the composition of the Stratford man's plays — how and exactly where and when he wrote them — is not likely to be solved, because the great dramatist was not given to explicit self-revelation, and no contemporary has told the story of his life and art. That he collaborated with one or more of his colleagues, particularly in his earliest and latest plays, we feel reasonably sure; that he furnished certain London theatres with a fairly steady succession of plays for something like twenty years, we know. How these comedies, histories, and tragedies passed from Shakespeare's to the actors' hands is a far more answerable question than one about their composition.

The producers of plays in Shakespeare's time were companies, or groups, of players. A number of these men banded themselves together under the patronage, or protection, of some nobleman for the purpose of presenting plays in a London theatre. As his "servants" they were not only free from interference by civic officials, but they won decided prestige from his name. The company, after being licensed by their patron, leased a playhouse and proceeded to conduct business on a cooperative basis, sharing expenses and dividing profits. They engaged boy apprentices, who acted the women's parts (no women acted in the public theatres until after the Restoration in 1660), and they hired assistants, such as stagehands and extras. Gifted apprentices might later become full-fledged members of the company, acting leading roles.

The company bought plays, either from a member who happened to be a playwright as well as an actor, or from a broker who made a business of buying and selling plays. The best known theatrical agent in London during Shakespeare's lifetime was Philip Henslowe, manager and owner of playhouses, whose diary, or account book, is a principal source of information on theatres, actors, and dramatists. Of the several dramatic companies the one of which Shakespeare was a member is the most famous. This was known in succession as Lord Strange's, Lord Derby's, Lord Hunsdon's, or the Lord Chamberlain's, according to the title or official position of its patron; but after the accession of James I in 1603, this company became "the King's men," acting under royal pa-

tronage. These men might be ordered to perform at the palace before the King, as they or
their predecessors had sometimes acted before
Queen Elizabeth. As Shakespeare belonged to
this group of players, he naturally wrote for
them. While composing a play he probably
read parts of it to his colleagues, perhaps in a
tavern near the playhouse, inviting criticism and
constructive suggestions. Thus the play itself
might be in a measure a collaborative product,
incorporating such practical ideas of the best
theatrical minds as the dramatist chose to accept.

By selling his play to the company the dramatist relinquished all rights in it. Once sold, the
play became the company's exclusive property
and might not be produced elsewhere or published without their consent. As a member of
the company Shakespeare became a sharer in
the profits of the plays produced, including his
own. Moreover, he might act in his own as well
as in other plays staged by the company. He is
said to have acted the Ghost in *Hamlet* and
Adam in *As You Like It* and also to have had a
part in two of Ben Jonson's plays. Since Shakespeare wrote his plays primarily for the stage
and generally for a particular group of players,
he must, in creating his characters, have had in

mind the actors who would speak the different parts of the dialogue. This will partly account for the variety of speeches in an Elizabethan play and the frequent introduction of a subplot in both tragedy and comedy. The gravediggers in *Hamlet*, the group of illiterate constables in *Much Ado*, the mob scenes in *Julius Caesar* and *Coriolanus*, the witches in *Macbeth*, and the various fools, or clowns, high and low, are illustrations of the mixture of types in the plays. In the list of the twenty-six members of Shakespeare's company recorded in the First Folio edition of the plays occur the names of most of the great actors of the day — Richard Burbage, William Kempe, William Slye, Robert Armin, and John Lowin. Richard Burbage excelled in tragedy and William Kempe in comedy. And in this company of players were Shakespeare's memorable friends, John Heminge and Henry Condell, who edited the first collection of his plays. Indeed, there was only one actor in another company, Edward Alleyn, who rivaled in reputation the great Burbage. It is evident, then, that Shakespeare had his hands full as a writer of plays to be acted by his colleagues and that his own acting was a secondary matter. His fellow players, on the contrary, were not dramatists, being content to "strut and fret" their

Nathaniel Field, a celebrated actor in Shakespeare's plays.
From an original picture in Dulwich College

hour upon the stage as interpreters of what others wrote.

Numerous references to the actor's art in the dramas of Shakespeare show his practical acquaintance with it. No one could so aptly have used stage terms without an extensive personal knowledge of the inside of a theatre gained from familiar association with players. Only an expert in the theory and practice of acting would have been able to put in Hamlet's mouth the advice to the group of traveling players about to perform before the King at Elsinore (Act III, scene 2). This speech is doubtless Shakespeare's own little lecture on the art of speaking lines, the keynote of which is moderation in tone and manner. He must have spoken feelingly when he warned the clowns not to indulge in wisecracks to raise a laugh, but to confine themselves to what was set down for them. No doubt the great dramatist had heard his own plays marred by what he was condemning.

The actors in an Elizabethan company learned their parts as copied from the manuscript furnished by the author to the company. Before it came into the company's hands it had been duly licensed by the public official known as the Master of the Revels, to whom was sub-

mitted the completed revision containing certain suggestions by members of the company.
It is not likely that the full text of a play was
retained in the acting copy, for a long play like
*Hamlet*, for instance, must have required considerable "cutting" to bring it within the usual
two-hour limit of the performance. There
were, then, Shakespeare's own manuscript, the
prompter's copy, and copies of their several
parts for the actors. The manuscripts, well
bound, were kept in the archives of the theatres,
which meant for Shakespeare's company the
Globe and the Blackfriars. The first Globe
Theatre burned in 1613 and with it may have
perished certain manuscripts and stage properties. In general, it may be said, either carelessness or fires in Elizabethan London caused the
loss of most dramatic documents. No manuscript of a Shakespeare play has come down to
us. The same is true, with few exceptions, of
the manuscripts of other Elizabethan writers.
We must content ourselves with copies of them
in printed editions.

How much an Elizabethan dramatist received for the manuscript of his play is a question provoked by natural curiosity. What did a
company or a broker pay the author for what
might prove to be an immortal contribution to

dramatic literature? According to Henslowe's *Diary* about £8 was the usual price. In modern monetary values this would be considerably more, varying from five to eight or ten times as much, as estimated by scholars. At any rate, the amount received by Shakespeare for a great play was absurdly small as compared with its stage and literary value in our eyes. The dramatist, unless he wrote a very great deal, could hardly support himself by writing plays. He might supplement his income from this source by sharing in the profits of his company, or as stockholder in a theatre, or as hackwriter, or as a beneficiary of noble or royal favor. And though his plays might be collected and published, it would probably be too late for him to reap any financial gain from them. His immediate reward as an artist was no doubt the inner satisfaction he enjoyed from the applause of the hearers as they watched with enthusiastic approval his characters on the stage.

William Kempe, the original performer of Dogberry in
*Much Ado about Nothing*

## HOW THE PLAYS WERE STAGED

A PLAYHOUSE in Shakespeare's time was
the product of a long development. Before the first regular London theatre was built
in 1576, plays had been acted in the courtyards
of inns; the stage, an improvised platform, was
at one end, before the door to the inner court,
with the audience filling the ground space and
the galleries, or balconies, into which the rooms
opened. This arrangement became a sort of
general model, or pattern, for later public play-

houses. The two earliest houses, the Theatre and the Curtain, were in the Shoreditch region northwest of the city proper. The newer theatres were south of the Thames, on the Bankside, also out of the city. These were the Globe, the Swan, the Rose, and the Hope. Besides these there were two others, the Fortune in Golding Lane, north of the city, and the Blackfriars in the city, regarded as a private theatre.

The public theatre was a three-story wooden building, round or nearly so. The Globe was octagonal. The Fortune, however, was square, eighty by eighty feet outside and fifty-five by fifty-five inside. The three tiers of seats were under a tiled or thatched roof, but the central space was open to the sky. Into this open area, where the "groundlings" stood, extended the stage, a platform either rectangular or tapering to the front. Around the edges of this in some theatres there seems to have been a railing to safeguard the players. Over a part of this projecting stage extended a roof, or "heavens," supported by two pillars, and above this roof, to the rear, rose the "hut," visible from the outside, in which there seems to have been machinery for lowering and raising deities and other figures necessary for the action of the play. Opening from the back of the stage into the dressing, or "tiring," room were two doors, and above the alcove between these doors was a narrow upper stage for use as the wall of a besieged city, or as a balcony, when a higher level was needed. When not used in the play this space might be occupied by spectators. Thus the typical stage of an Elizabethan play-house may be visualized as consisting of an outer stage on which most of the action took place, an inner stage which might be curtained off, and an elevated stage. Only the inner stage was protected from the weather by the project-ing "heavens." Performances were in the after-noon, beginning about two o'clock and lasting two hours. In the winter the public theatres would be closed. There was no artificial light, though torches might be used to give the illu-sion of night happenings. The private theatres, such as the Blackfriars, where there were night performances, were of course lighted, and their stage and seating arrangements were naturally different.

Elizabethan theatres had no scenery in the modern sense, but stage properties were them-selves often scenic in effect. Benches, chairs, beds, shrubs, branches of trees, and the like were used on the outer stage, while the inner, or alcove, stage might with slight adjustment

Interior of the Globe Theatre, from the model in the
Folger Shakespeare Library, Washington, D. C.

be transformed into a cave (*Cymbeline*), a prison (*Richard II, Twelfth Night*), a cell (*The Tempest*), a tomb (*Romeo and Juliet*). Scenes requiring out-of-door stage properties will readily come to mind: the moving forest in *Macbeth*, Portia's garden at Belmont, screening shrubbery in *Twelfth Night* and *Much Ado*. Stirring scenes such as shipwrecks and battles could not of course be realistically represented, but even without scenery swift, confused movement, vivid descriptive speeches, and noise back of the stage would conjure up pictures in the hearers' imaginations. Somewhere in the floor of the outer stage and sometimes of the back stage, there was a trap door through which might be propelled from below a demon or a ghost; and when an open grave was required, the gravediggers might be exposed waist-deep in the "earth" jesting with each other as they threw up a skull from an old grave about to be occupied by another tenant. Such a spectacular play as *A Midsummer Night's Dream* certainly demanded a variety of properties, and the Masque of Ceres in *The Tempest* must have required extraordinary activity by stagehands, lowering, suspending, and elevating the various deities with some sort of mechanism worked from the hut above. The following brief stage direction in the last act of *Cymbeline* is another illustration of this: *Jupiter descends in thunder and lightning, sitting upon an eagle. He throws a thunderbolt.*

The limitations of the Elizabethan stage in size and properties were fully recognized by Shakespeare, and he sometimes exhorts the spectators to use their imaginations. His most striking appeal to this effect is the apologetic prologue in *Henry V*, a play which represents heroic battle episodes:

> But pardon, gentles all,
> The flat unraised spirits that have dared
> On this unworthy scaffold to bring forth
> So great an object. Can this cockpit hold
> The vasty fields of France? Or may we cram
> Within this wooden O the very casques
> That did affright the air at Agincourt? . . .
> Piece out our imperfections with your thoughts;
> Into a thousand parts divide one man
> And make imaginary puissance.
> Think, when we talk of horses, that you see them
> Printing their proud hoofs i' th' receiving earth.
> For 'tis your thoughts that now must deck our
> kings.

The bareness of the Shakespearean stage, compared to the later elaborateness in scenery and furniture, was no great handicap in getting the story across to the audience if the acting was good. Indeed, it is remarkable how realistically an old play will go on a modern stage, bare of scenery, or with only "symbolical" equipment, when the players follow Shakespeare's advice as spoken to them by Hamlet. Though poor in scenery the Elizabethan stage was rich in the pictorial effect of players' costumes. These were elaborate, costly, and often gorgeous. One garment sometimes cost as much as the dramatist received for the play. Stage dress was generally Elizabethan, and a lady or gentleman of the period garbed in court attire was a colorful sight. Imagine Shakespeare's kings and queens, lords and ladies, moving about on a platform, bare except for a throne and a chair or so, and you will hardly miss the scenery. Or fill the stage with a ragged, milling mob, enlivened by a street fight, and you will have spectacle enough without artificial decoration. There was no attempt at historical accuracy in dress and surroundings. Julius Caesar and Mark Antony were arrayed like Elizabethan generals; eleventh-century Lady Macbeth was impersonated by a boy dressed up like Mary Queen of Scots; and the dress of a thirteenth- or fourteenth-century king was like that of his reigning majesty James I. Such was the anachronistic costuming of principal characters; but lesser persons in the play, such as shepherds and shepherdesses, mythological figures, and fools, appeared in accepted conventional dress. The dress of royalty had doubtless become standardized. The audience apparently liked to see the actors in garments familiar to them in the frequent processions and festivals of the day.

What made an Elizabethan play successful was not primarily its appeal to the eye, important as that was, but its appeal to the ear. A play was and is to be heard *and* seen. Well-spoken lines will make up for scenery. The reading aloud of Shakespearean speeches will often make clear what in a silent reading is obscure. Perhaps the very lack of scenery made the actors of Shakespeare's day use their voices to greatest advantage. Hamlet, when lecturing the players on practical dramatics, insisted that they speak "trippingly on the tongue" as he pronounced the speech to them, taking care not to "mouth" their words.

The audience in a public theatre was a varied assemblage. The standing groundlings in the pit, restless unless the show entertained them, might manifest their displeasure by throwing things at the players. Since the stage projected far into the pit, these lower spectators were quite close to the actors on three sides, and this nearness of hearer to speaker makes an "aside" or soliloquy seem more natural than it does on the more remote picture-frame stage of today. Near to the players, also, were the showily dressed gallants, who sometimes sat on the sides of the platform and by their remarks and movements proved annoying both to actors and audience. Beyond and above all these were the galleries, or balconies, occupied by the more substantial, well-to-do citizens. To such an audience of lower and higher folk, of uncultured and cultured, a Shakespearean play must appeal. The groundling, who paid a penny for admission, and the prosperous tradesman or nobleman who was comfortable in his higher-priced seat, must each find enjoyment in the performance, whether he could understand everything or not. In the private theatres, in the halls of the nobility and at court, with smaller and more refined audiences, the acting may have been somewhat different; probably some of the more highly colored speeches were omitted and possibly certain ribald passages toned down, though the Elizabethans, high and low, were not opposed to coarseness. At any rate, a play had to please all sorts. This variety

of interest, this wide appeal, is of course one of
the most extraordinary things about a Shakespearean play.

There was little or no delay between the
acts. Indeed, strict act division, as later indicated in published editions of plays, was not
always observed in the earlier acting versions.
The performance went straight on, unless there
was music or a pause for change of properties.
The numerous songs in Shakespeare's plays sat-
isfied the Elizabethans' love of music, brought
a change of tone, or atmosphere, and so made
a welcome break in the action. Transition from
one locality to another was sometimes indicated
by a placard, or by a speaker — as when Rosalind says, "This is the forest of Arden" — but
the audience was not concerned about historical and geographical accuracy. They no doubt
anglicized places and plots, with London as
capital and sixteenth-century English customs
as universal. In *Hamlet*, which is presumably
being acted in the early Danish capital of Elsinore, Rosencrantz remarks to the Prince of
Denmark (II, 2) that the traveling company of
players, just arrived, are "the tragedians of the
city" who have taken to the (English) provinces because the children's companies are now
in possession of the regular (London) theatres,

including the Globe! Such an anachronism gave an Elizabethan audience no trouble.

As there was no curtain to the outer stage, some device was necessary for indicating to the audience the termination of a scene and for the graceful exit of the players. The closing lines of a speech in ringing couplets, stirring the audience to applause, might indicate this. Macbeth, hard pressed by his foes and by signs of his approaching fate, gives orders for his last stand:

> Ring the alarum-bell! — Blow, wind! come, wrack!
> At least we'll die with harness on our back.

And he strides off the stage with climactic effect. The final scene in a tragedy might close with a funeral procession and in a comedy with a dance. Or there might be a formal epilogue, spoken by one of the characters. Getting the actors off a curtainless stage through the back doors was probably not so awkward a proceeding to an Elizabethan audience as it would be to a modern one. The actors' retirement from the inner stage could be hidden by the drawn curtains.

Few pictures of the Elizabethan theatre have

Interior of the Swan Theatre in 1596. A contemporary
drawing by Johannes De Witt

survived, but from these, from existing build-ers' contracts, and from stage directions we get a fairly accurate idea of the outside and the inside of a Shakespearean playhouse. Vischer's *View of London* in 1616 (the year of Shake-speare's death) shows the Swan and second Globe theatres on the Bankside; Speed's Atlas of 1611 shows the circular Rose playhouse in the same region. A sketch of the interior of the Swan by a visiting Dutchman (Johannes De Witt) in 1596 is the only contemporary draw-ing, but the builder's contract for the Fortune is the basis of the reconstruction of that theatre. Mid-seventeenth century views of the interior of two theatres, showing a tapering, railed plat-form, have been helpful in descriptions of the Elizabethan stage. From all these sources, supplemented by information from the plays themselves, we get a good general notion of how these plays were staged in a public play-house.

Windsor Castle across the river Thames. Eton College at the left, where classical plays were acted

# HOW THE PLAYS
## GOT INTO PRINT

TODAY we regard Shakespeare's plays as literature, to be read or studied and occasionally to be seen on the stage. They have become classics which scholars edit for the student and the general reader. And so we are apt to get the impression that Shakespeare wrote his plays for reading or study and that, in composing them, he had his eyes on the future. If he did, he was strangely indifferent about preserving them, as will be shown later. Equally indifferent were most of that large group of Elizabethan playwrights who furnished companies of actors with material for their popular profession. The fact is, Shakespeare and his fellow dramatists wrote directly for the stage, with little or no thought of publication. If any such idea occurred to them, it was probably an afterthought. Their immediate purpose was to write a play which had a practical acting value.

While Shakespeare, so far as we know, did not express himself on the nature and purpose of dramatic creation, some of his contemporary craftsmen did. John Marston, in a statement in the preface to one of his published plays, assures the reader that "comedies are writ to be spoken, not read," and urges him to "remember, the life of these things consists in action." John Webster, in the preface to one of his tragedies, speaks of plays as having no literary importance (*"nos haec novimus esse nil* — we know these things are of no value"), and apologizes for publishing them. Indeed, the conception of a play as a short-lived kind of entertainment rather than literature long persisted. When Ben Jonson collected and published his plays in 1616 as *The Works of Benjamin Jonson*, he became the subject of ironic comment among his fellow dramatists, who had great sport with him for calling them "works." Thomas Heywood, for instance, smugly declared: "My plays are not exposed to the world in volumes to bear the title of *Works*, as others." And elsewhere occurs this satirical question, addressed to the old classicist:

Pray, tell me, Ben, where does the mystery lurk,
What others call a *play*, you call a *work?*

We find the same attitude toward Shakespeare's published plays. After they had become well known in the great Folio collection, a popular dramatist made Captain Underwrit, the chief character in his comedy of that name, speak thus:

"Shakespeare's *works!* Why Shakespeare's *works?* . . . They are plays." Evidently the impression prevailed that a play was a rapidly written composition, entailing no such laborious effort and learning as a *work* (such as a history or a treatise) and therefore not entitled to be dignified by the name of literature. So much for the light esteem in which plays were held.

Let us consider next why and how they got into print. What delayed their publication was primarily a commercial consideration. If a play were printed, its rightful owners, the company of actors in a certain theatre, feared that it might be presented in a rival playhouse. If a play were available to the public in printed form, those who read it might not care to see it. In either case, the company owning it would lose money. When, however, certain plays began to appear in print, often in imperfect form, the authors might be as much concerned as the owners, but for a different reason. If the play were published, the author would naturally want it textually correct. The dramatist Heywood, in the preface to one of his plays, feelingly asserts that he has never been guilty of selling a play both to the theatre and to the press, and that he would not publish his plays except for his desire to correct the "corrupt and mangled" version ("coppied only by the eare"). The permission to print an authentic copy he doubtless received from the owners of the manuscript, the theatrical company.

The only legitimate way in which a play might come into the printer's hands was either by outright purchase from the owning company or through their gracious permission to the author to publish. Another, and apparently not uncommon, way was through some person in the audience who took down the speeches of the actors in shorthand. Heywood has something to say on this method in one of his prologues: the audience, he says,

Did throng the seats, the boxes, and the stage
So much, that some by stenography drew
The plot, put it in print, scarce one word true.

It was also possible for a dishonest actor to sell
his own part of the dialogue and as much of the
other parts as he could remember; or some hireling of the company might get one player's
speeches, add to them, and dispose of the patch-
work. By the first, or legitimate, method the
author's manuscript or the promptbook, both
presumably in the storeroom of the theatre,
would be the source of the printing and would
assure accuracy of text for the complete play.
By the second or third method there would, of
course, be furnished the printer an incomplete
or imperfect copy.

The protests of a few dramatists against the
publication of imperfect versions, and their
prompt efforts to issue authentic copies, show
a trend toward the recognition of a play as
something to be read as well as seen and heard.
Tragedies were more in the literary tradition
than comedies, for the models of much Elizabethan tragedy were in the classical inheritance
of the English Renaissance, but both forms
were on the way to the library shelves. Dedications in the form of addresses *To the Reader*,

prefixed to the authors' authentic versions, indicate that henceforth the dramatist had to
reckon with the reader as well as with the
spectator.

In the absence of a copyright law both authors and publishers must have some protection
against illegal printing. For this purpose a play
had to be officially licensed and then recorded
in the register of the Stationers' Company of
London printers and publishers. In a commercial way the publishers would, of course, profit
more by the protection afforded by such registration than the author, for the latter had no
longer any ownership rights in his plays. The
process, then, through which, ideally at least, a
play had to pass from author to printer was,
first, approval for stage presentation by the
Master of the Revels; second, licensing for publication by an ecclesiastical or other official; and
third, registration, on payment of a small fee,
in the Stationers' Company. This was no doubt
the general practice, but in spite of care by
licensers and stationers, pirated copies of plays
managed to get into print.

Shakespeare seems to have had no direct hand
in the publication of his plays. This may have
been because, as already intimated, plays were
not held in high esteem as literature, or, indeed,

as literature at all. It is hard to believe, however, that Shakespeare, artist and poet as he was, could have been unaware of the literary quality of his dramas, or that his modesty was so great as to prevent his publishing them. One can hardly think so; but one thing is certain, namely, that he had no such high estimate of his creations as Jonson had of his own "works." A more convincing explanation of Shakespeare's failure to publish his dramas is to be found in the fact that he no longer owned them, having disposed of his rights in them to the theatrical company. And the company probably would not part with the manuscript as long as the plays paid on the stage. It is as interesting as it is futile to speculate on whether Shakespeare, had he lived longer, would have collected and published his plays. Fortunately, others soon began to realize their value for readers and proceeded to get a number of them published in the author's lifetime.

There were sixteen of the plays printed at intervals from 1594 to 1609. Each was a slender volume in quarto form, and they are known to us collectively as the Shakespeare Quartos. Five of these little books are called bad quartos because they were evidently printed from stenographic or other incomplete, corrupted copies.

The most famous of the bad group is the First Quarto of *Hamlet* (1603) which, as an outstanding example of textual imperfection, invites a few words of comment. This quarto, like one of Shakespeare's kings, came into the world "so deformed, unfinished, and scarce half made up" that critics have barked at it for many years. It is only about half as long as the excellent Second Quarto of *Hamlet;* important passages are omitted, others inverted, and scenes mixed, so that we are presented with a general hodgepodge of characters and dialogue. Some theatrical hireling probably made up the text from the play as he, a poor stenographer, took it down from the mouths of the actors, later introducing lines of his own (he was certainly no poet!) when his memory failed him. The other bad quartos are those of *Romeo and Juliet, The Merry Wives of Windsor, Henry V,* and *Pericles* (a play partly by Shakespeare). These defective imprints were later displaced by more authentic texts either in quarto or folio.

The other eleven of the sixteen plays are the good quartos, presumably taken from the manuscripts in the playhouse and fully authorized. They are *Titus Andronicus* (the first of Shakespeare's plays to be published), *Richard II,*

# A
# Midſommer nights
## dreame.

As it hath beene ſundry times pub-
lickely acted, by the Right honoura-
ble, the Lord Chamberlaine his
ſeruants.

*Written by William Shakeſpeare.*

¶ Imprinted at London, for *Thomas Fiſher*, and are to
be ſoulde at his ſhoppe, at the Signe of the White Hart,
in *Fleeteſtreete.* 1 6 0 0.

The title page of the quarto edition of *A Midsummer
Night's Dream*, 1600

*Richard III, Henry IV* (in two parts), *Love's
Labour's Lost, The Merchant of Venice,
Henry V, Much Ado about Nothing, A Midsummer Night's Dream, King Lear,* and *Troilus
and Cressida.* Shakespeare did not live to see
any more of his plays in print. Whether he
helped in any way with their publication, or
what his sentiments were on seeing these brain
children of his in literary dress, we do not
know. It is probably fair to assume, however,
that he was annoyed at the bad quartos, particularly the imperfect *Hamlet,* for the very
next year (1604) a good quarto of that play appeared; he may have taken a hand in the matter
himself. Six years after Shakespeare's death a
quarto of *Othello* was published (1622), and a
year later the great collection known as the
First Folio made practically all his plays available to readers.

Before this, in 1619, a certain London publisher, Thomas Pavier, conceived the idea of
printing a collection of Shakespearean plays,
including several wrongly attributed to the
great dramatist, which he managed by fair
means or foul to get into his possession. But before he could print his proposed volume of ten
plays (six of which were Shakespeare's in
whole or part) he had to give up his scheme,

probably because of the opposition of the company of actors, who still owned some of them, and of one or more of Shakespeare's noble patrons. Balked in his plan to publish a single volume, Pavier actually issued the plays separately in quarto form. This attempt at a collected edition of some of Shakespeare's dramas may have been suggested by Ben Jonson's volume of nine of his plays three years before. The project, however, had to wait several years until two of Shakespeare's friends and fellow actors realized it on a large and notable scale.

These two men were John Heminge and Henry Condell, already mentioned as members of Shakespeare's company of players. They had known the great dramatist well, and now wished to collect and publish his plays "without ambition of self-profit or fame," to quote their own words, "only to keep the memory of so worthy a friend and fellow alive." Their undertaking, then, was a labor of love in honor of their dead colleague who, it is intimated, would have published his own plays had he lived. This purpose is set forth in the dedication of the volume to the Earls of Pembroke and of Montgomery, Shakespeare's noble friends. Thus was issued in 1623, seven years after the author's death, the First Folio, or collection, of Shake-

speare's plays. It is the most significant achieve-
ment in the history of English dramatic literature. This volume is now the most valuable
secular book in the world. With its appearance
Shakespeare's fame was assured. The man of
Stratford had become one of the immortals.

The First Folio is a volume of slightly over
nine hundred pages, thirteen by eight inches
($13\frac{3}{8}$ by $8\frac{1}{2}$ in the largest extant copy), printed
in double columns. The frontispiece is Droe-
shout's engraving, or woodcut, of Shakespeare.
Two London printers, Isaac Jaggard and Edward Blunt, brought out the work. Facing the
picture of the dramatist are Ben Jonson's lines
testifying to its genuineness. Of the four poetic
tributes that follow, Ben Jonson's is outstanding; it is the noblest praise bestowed upon any
Elizabethan dramatist by a fellow poet. Only a
few lines may be quoted here, those forming
the invocation:

> Soul of the Age!
> The Applause! delight! the wonder of our Stage!
> My Shakespeare, rise: I will not lodge thee by
> Chaucer, or Spenser, or bid Beaumont lye
> A little further to make thee a roome:
> Thou art a Moniment without a tombe,
> And art alive still, while thy Booke doth live,
> And we have wits to read, and praise to give.

The First Folio contains thirty-six plays, "published," the editors assert, "according to the True Originall Copies," which probably means the playhouse manuscripts. The collection begins with *The Tempest* and ends with *Cymbeline*. The plays are divided into Comedies, Histories, and Tragedies, an easy but not perfectly accurate classification. *The Tempest* may have been put first, as Professor Hazelton Spencer suggests, because it was a favorite play at the time and had never before been printed. It would be difficult to say just what determined the order of the plays in the First Folio, and one feels that a particular play may have been thrust into a certain place for reasons best known to the printers. The typography of the volume is sometimes eccentric or confused; this may have been due to illegibility or variations in the manuscript used by the printers. Elizabethan spelling was quite variable and punctuation very uncertain. Of the thirty-six plays in the Folio twenty were published for the first time, and for these the Folio text is the sole authority; the others had, as already stated, appeared in quarto. The large volume sold for one pound, and it has been estimated that five or six hundred copies were printed. Between one hundred and fifty and two hundred of these are still in existence. The few perfect copies are, of course, among the world's almost priceless books.

The Second Folio, following the text of the First, was printed in 1632; the Third appeared in 1663 and was reprinted the next year with the play of *Pericles*, and six plays attributed to Shakespeare, added; and in 1685 the Fourth Folio. Each Folio is a reprint of the preceding, with its many errors but with some attempted corrections. This ended the published collections of the plays before the eighteenth century, though quarto editions of certain plays were reprinted from time to time. All that we have of Shakespeare's plays and poems were now available to readers who could afford to pay for them. The next step was the editing of his "works" for the reader and the scholar; and with this begins that long line of Shakespearean editors and critics, which, like the line of Macbeth's royal apparitions, seems to stretch out to the crack of doom.

*Henry IV* in the nineteenth century — Hotspur and Prince Henry. From a daguerreotype

# HOW THE PLAYS
## BECAME "CLASSICS"

THE most famous literary and dramatic critic in Shakespeare's own lifetime and for twenty years after was Ben Jonson, and we have seen how highly he thought of Shakespeare. Jonson, who had the classicist's sense of restraint, had only one critical comment to make on his friend's art, namely, that it showed a sort of fluent freedom: "he flowed with that facility that sometimes it was necessary he should be stopped." That remark may be regarded as a forecast of much of the critical opinion of Shakespeare in the later seventeenth century. Influenced by the neoclassical standards of that time, which stressed form and "regularity" in literature, many critics thought Shakespeare an irregular genius given to extravagance in matter and manner. The most violent of these dramatic critics was Thomas Rymer, who declared that "there is more meaning and expression in the neighing of a horse or the growling of a mastiff than in Shakespeare's tragical flights." Rymer, like other Restoration sticklers for regularity and mediocrity, wanted Shakespeare "toned down." Even the great Milton, who had glorified Shakespeare in some memorable lines first published in the Second Folio, referred to him a little later as "warbling his native woodnotes wild." This charge of "wildness" against the Elizabethans was fairly common among the classical-minded of the succeeding age.

But this was by no means the general view of Shakespeare in the seventeenth century. The sanest, most representative, and certainly the most discriminating opinion of him was that of John Dryden who, in his able essay on "Dramatic Poesy" (1668), expressed himself thus:

He was the man who of all modern, and
perhaps ancient poets, had the largest and
most comprehensive soul. All the images of
nature were still present to him, and he drew
them, not laboriously, but luckily; when he
describes anything, you more than see it, you
feel it too. Those who accuse him to have
wanted learning, give him the greater com-
mendation: he was naturally learned; he
needed not the spectacles of books to read
nature; he looked inwards, and found her
there. I cannot say he is everywhere alike;
were he so, I should do him injury to compare him with the greatest of mankind. He is
many times flat, insipid; his comick wit de-
generating into clenches [puns], his serious,
swelling into bombast. But he is always great
when some great occasion is presented to
him.

And Dryden goes on to say that the dramatic
contemporaries of Shakespeare, such as Beaumont, Fletcher, and Jonson, were not in their
own time held equal to him. Dryden further
remarks that "when Ben's reputation was at
highest, Sir John Suckling, and with him the
greater part of the courtiers, set our Shakespeare far above him."

Dryden mentions two of what seventeenth-

century critics regarded as faults in Shakespeare's plays: (1) the frequent lack of eleva-
tion in tone, as shown in punning and other
forms of wordplay; and (2) the use of flowery
speech "swelling into bombast." Other violations of classical dramatic tradition were Shakespeare's mixture of the serious and the comic,
his disregard of the unities of time and place,
his irregularity of plot structure, and his occasional obscurity arising from the use of obso-
lete words or from faulty sentence structure.
These charges show that tastes and conditions
had changed since the spacious days of Elizabethan England. Not only the critics but the
public wanted a different sort of drama. In
comedy they preferred the social comedy of
manners with its brilliant dialogue, but without action; in serious drama they liked the so-
called heroic tragedy with its rhyming couplets and its dominating superman, unrelieved
by anything "low" or trivial. But along with all
this drawing-room comedy and this sound-and-
fury tragedy, Shakespeare's plays were still
acted and read. And though their essential truth
to life was recognized, the changed conditions
of the Restoration stage demanded that the
great dramatist's plays, particularly certain
tragedies, should be modified to suit contempo-

rary taste, which was thought to be more refined than that of a more "barbarous" age.

Several of the tragedies suffered radical al-
terations. Davenant revised *Macbeth* by introducing new scenes of dancing and witches.
Howard changed *Romeo and Juliet* into a
tragi-comedy, ending happily. Nahum Tate,
late seventeenth-century poet laureate, furnished a happy ending to *King Lear* by restoring the old king to his throne and betrothing
Cordelia and Edgar, a monstrous perversion of
the play which proved popular for over a century. Colley Cibber, actor and playwright, revised *Richard III*, rewriting much of the play.
The now famous speech, "Richard's himself
again," is not Shakespeare's but Cibber's. Davenant and Dryden turned *The Tempest* into a
musical comedy, which is a grotesque travesty
of the play. But Dryden paid Shakespeare the
flattery of imitation in matter and blank verse
by writing a good play on Antony and Cleopatra which he called *All for Love*. The two
plays which escaped radical changes in all this
dramatic tinkering were *Hamlet* and *Othello*.

This attention to Shakespeare's plays, though
often harmful and destructive, was of course a
tribute to their enduring qualities. If popular
taste did not demand Shakespeare pure and un-

defiled, it at least regarded him as indispensable in some form. Testimony to an unbroken Shakespearean succession in the London theatres in the early Restoration period is furnished by Samuel Pepys in his *Diary*. Pepys, a constant theatregoer, recorded his impressions of certain plays which he saw either in the original or in revised versions. *Hamlet* he saw five times, *Macbeth* nine, and *The Tempest* eight. He was present at one or more performances of twelve Shakespeare plays in forty productions. He pronounces *A Midsummer Night's Dream* insipid and ridiculous and *Twelfth Night* weak and silly. The truth is, Restoration patrons of the theatre did not care for romantic comedy, preferring the urban social realism of Congreve to the poetic sentiment of the Forest of Arden or an enchanted island. It does not seem surprising, therefore, that to a generation avowedly unromantic the most popular Shakespearean comedy was *The Merry Wives of Windsor*.

The later seventeenth century had several great actors and actresses, for women were now playing on the public stage. The actor who carried on most brilliantly the traditions of the Elizabethan Burbage was Thomas Betterton, playing Hamlet, Othello, Macbeth, and

other leading parts in tragedy. Mrs. Betterton
and the beautiful Mrs. Bracegirdle acted the
feminine parts. Betterton, who was a student of
theatrical conditions in Elizabethan England,
created a tradition in Shakespearean roles which
lasted far into the next century. He was succeeded by the eminent Irish actor, Charles
Macklin, who gave a more human and sympa-
thetic interpretation of Shylock. The most famous actor of the eighteenth century, and one
of the greatest of all time, was David Garrick.
Garrick may be called the first modern actor,
for his impersonations of Shakespearean characters were far more natural in tone and manner than those of his predecessors. Playing with
Garrick in his final appearance as Richard III
was Sarah Siddons, who had the part of Lady
Anne. Mrs. Siddons was the greatest tragic
actress of her day, which extended into the
nineteenth century, and her acting of Lady
Macbeth is one of the finest traditions of the
English stage.

The line of distinguished Shakespearean actors and actresses of the nineteenth century is
a long one. It includes the Kembles, Edmund
Kean (famous as Richard III, Hamlet, Othello,
and King Lear), Macready, Sir Henry Irving,
Ellen Terry, Forbes-Robertson; and in Amer-

ica, Junius Brutus Booth, Edwin Forrest, and Edwin Booth, the last the greatest of American Shakespearean actors. Those who once saw Booth in *Hamlet* can never forget his distinguished presence, his glorious eyes with their haunting melancholy, and his deep, musical voice. And so the acting of Shakespeare has gone on in an unbroken succession, varying in manner and method from generation to generation, but with continuing appeal to high and low.

For almost one hundred years after Shakespeare's death the Folios and Quartos were the only editions of the plays. These continued to be used by players, with such changes as the public taste demanded, and by an increasing number of readers. Most of the textual corruptions in the earlier Folios had been continued in the last, or Fourth Folio of 1685, and in the reprinted Quartos. The acting versions of a few plays, as we have seen, had been so extensively rewritten as to be only faintly Shakespearean. Not, indeed, until well on in the eighteenth century, under Garrick's influence, were these stage versions of Shakespeare partially restored. Meanwhile, Shakespeare's popularity and fame had grown enormously until he had well nigh eclipsed the other Elizabethan dramatists. By

A scene from *The Taming of the Shrew*. From Rowe's
illustrated edition of Shakespeare, 1709

the beginning of the eighteenth century he had become a classic. But there was need of a new edition of all his plays in a corrected and modernized text, with explanatory notes and other helps to a better understanding of the dramatist. Thus began the long line of modern Shakespearean editors.

The first modern editor of Shakespeare was Nicholas Rowe, dramatist and poet laureate, who published in 1709 his six-volume edition of the plays. The title page reads: *The Works of Mr. William Shakespear; in Six Volumes. Adorned with Cuts. Revised and Corrected, with an Account of the Life and Writings of the Author. By N. Rowe, Esq.* The following year Rowe added a seventh volume containing the nondramatic poems. In 1714 he published a revised edition in eight volumes. Both editions included the six plays wrongly attributed to Shakespeare. The text was largely that of the Fourth Folio, with a number of corrections. Aside from these Rowe made some valuable contributions. One of these was the biographical sketch of Shakespeare, with appreciative comments on his plots and characters, prefixed to the first volume. Another was his annotation of the plays. A further contribution was the adding of character lists to many plays which had none in the Folios; and still another was the division into acts and scenes of those six plays which lacked them and of the thirteen which were only partly supplied with them. Moreover, he modernized punctuation and spelling, added stage directions, and rearranged certain confused passages into correct verse form.

Alexander Pope, following Rowe's text, published his edition of Shakespeare in 1725 in six handsome volumes. He eliminated *Pericles* and the six spurious plays, rejected certain passages regarded as "unworthy" of Shakespeare, improved the verse here and there according to contemporary taste, and explained, sometimes wrongly, many textual obscurities. Better as a critic than as an editor, Pope aroused the ire of Lewis Theobald (pronounced tibbald), an accomplished scholar, who promptly attacked the popular poet, exposing his editorial sins of omission and commission. For this Pope satirized him in his *Dunciad*, a common purgatory for his critics. Theobald was the first really competent Shakespearean editor, equipped as he was with extensive knowledge of Elizabethan literature, including a familiarity with the First Folio and the earlier Quartos. In his edition (1734) Theobald made many corrections of difficult passages. The most famous, and certainly the happiest, of these was his change of a meaningless phrase in Mrs. Quickly's account of the death of Falstaff (Henry V, ii, 3) — "and a table of greene fields" — into "and a [he] babbled of green fields," presumably a reminiscence on the part of the dying Falstaff of the "green pastures" of the twenty-third Psalm, familiar to him in childhood. This is now generally accepted as one of Theobald's many apt corrections of inaccurate texts.

Another outstanding Shakespearean editor of the same century was Dr. Samuel Johnson who, in the Preface to his edition (1765), contributed the first comprehensive essay on Shakespeare's work and genius. Johnson's commonsense interpretations in felicitous phrasing, rather than his scholarship, made his dramatic criticism memorable. It is the soundness of it rather than the depth which continues to appeal. His defense of Shakespeare's violation of the unities, for instance, has become a classic bit of reasoning. After Johnson the most notable eighteenth-century editor was Edmund Malone, who had already contributed an essay on Shakespearean chronology to the second edition of Johnson. Malone brought out his ten-volume edition in 1790; this reveals a wide knowledge of original documents and painstaking care in restoring the text. He was the pioneer in attempts to determine the order of the composition of the plays.

In the nineteenth century Shakespearean editors and critics were numerous, and in the twentieth their name is legion. By the nineteenth century there had accumulated in libraries and archives a considerable collection of Shakespeareana; since then Shakespearean bibliographies would fill volumes. Many of the writings about Shakespeare have themselves become classics. So extensive, indeed, is the writing *about* Shakespeare that the reading of the dramatist himself may be neglected. As is the case with other standard writers, the critical and interpretative comment may absorb the reader's whole attention and lead him to the conclusion that the play itself is of minor importance. Certainly there is no end of editions and no end of helps to an understanding of the master. As for Shakespearean scholarship, that has made enormous strides. And the materials for the study of Shakespeare are easily available in the historical and critical introductions of well-edited, one-volume collections of plays. If one wishes to see early editions and documents, as well as some of the editing and discussion of later scholars, there is no more fascinating place for the lover of Shakespeare than the monumental Folger Shakespeare Library in Washington.

A French knight mounts his horse before the Battle of Agincourt. From Olivier's photoplay, *Henry V*

# HOW THE PLAYS ARE CLASSIFIED

IN what order did Shakespeare write his plays? The question is important in tracing the dramatist's development as well as in the interpretation of the plays themselves. The Folios, as we have seen, do not answer this question, for the arrangement in them is certainly not chronological. The history plays, for instance, are grouped in the Folios in accordance with the historic time of the kings involved, beginning with John and ending with Henry VIII, and not according to the dates of composition. Two more illustrations of a different kind may be given. If you should carefully read the first two plays in the Folios, or in later editions following their order, namely, *The Tempest* and *The Two Gentlemen of Verona*, you would very likely feel that while the same man wrote both, he was a maturer man when he wrote *The Tempest*. *The Tempest*, you might conclude, could not be called Shakespeare's first play although put first. When you find *Titus Andronicus* and *Romeo and Juliet* toward the end of the Folio, you may well wonder why these early plays of the Quartos were placed so far along in the volume. Such obvious violations of chronological order led scholars, from the days of Malone, to seek to determine the true sequence in the writing of the plays. In this effort to rearrange the plays in the order of their composition, scholars have relied upon three kinds of evidence: external, internal-external, and internal.

External evidence would be the mention of a play by some contemporary of Shakespeare, or the occurrence of the name on the title page of the earliest Quarto, or an official record of its performance, or its entry for publication in the Stationers' Register. The twelve plays listed by Meres in his *Palladis Tamia* (1598) had of

course been written before that date and acted
still earlier. There is mention of a performance
of *Twelfth Night* at the Middle Temple on
February 2, 1602. All the plays recorded in the
Stationers' Register, with dates from 1594 to
1608, were ready for publication. All such evidence enables us to hit upon the approximate,
but not the exact, date of composition.

Internal-external evidence is a reference in
the play itself to some event outside the play
which is known to the hearer or reader. Perhaps the most definite reference in the plays to
a contemporary event is that in the prologue to
the fifth act of *Henry V*, where mention is
made of the expected triumphant return of the
Earl of Essex from his expedition to Ireland in
the spring and summer of 1599. Essex left for
Ireland March 27 and returned in defeat Sep-
tember 28. Somewhere, then, between these
dates the play was written. Other allusions in
the plays — in *Romeo and Juliet* to an earth-
quake, in *King Lear* to recent eclipses, and in
*A Midsummer Night's Dream* to a rainy summer — have been regarded by some scholars as
internal-external evidence of the date of writing. Manifestly, however, many allusions are
too vague and general to be convincing.

Internal evidence for arranging the plays in

groups as early, middle, or late is that found in the style, thought, and versification. Style is a subtle and variable quality, depending upon a writer's personality as well as upon the subject and the occasion; and we cannot be certain that the style, or manner of expression, in a given play accurately reveals the age of the writer at the time of its composition. In general, however, the tone and subject matter of a piece of dramatic writing are likely to vary somewhat in the several stages of a growing author's literary life. If you were to read all of Shakespeare's comedies or tragedies in fairly rapid succession, you would feel a marked difference between, let us say, *The Comedy of Errors* and *Twelfth Night* (both dealing in mistaken identity), or between *Richard III* and *Hamlet* (essentially one-man plays). The first of each of these two plays is full of action, declamatory in manner, and rather mechanical in structure; the second moves more slowly, is more restrained and thoughtful, and more varied in development. You would probably conclude that *The Comedy of Errors* and *Richard III* were written by a younger man than the other two, and if you had to classify them you would put them among Shakespeare's early plays.

On examining more closely these and additional plays you would find in some a noteworthy use of puns, conceits, and other tricks of speech. In still others you would come across sentences so burdened with thought or so condensed or so rambling that more than one reading would be necessary for their comprehension. And it is likely that the wordplay, figurative language, regularity of movement, and frequency of rhyme would impress you as youthful or even amateurish, while the more thoughtful and "difficult" reading would show mastery and perhaps serenity in the author. These considerations, along with more practical forms of evidence, have influenced scholars in the determination of the order in which Shakespeare's plays were written.

More measurable, however, than this stylistic evidence is the matter of versification. The blank verse of the plays is broken by frequent rhyming couplets and occasional lyrics, and in certain comedies there is a good deal of prose. The verse of *The Comedy of Errors, Romeo and Juliet*, and *Richard III* is far more regular than that in *The Winter's Tale, Cymbeline*, and *The Tempest*. The verse of the last three plays often resembles prose except for an underlying rhythm, and there are hardly any

Mr. WILLIAM

# SHAKESPEARES

COMEDIES,
HISTORIES, &
TRAGEDIES.

Publiſhed according to the True Originall Copies.

*Martin Droeſhout ſculpſit London.*

*LONDON*
Printed by Iſaac Iaggard, and Ed. Blount. 1623.

The title page of the First Folio, 1623

rhyming couplets. In the first three plays there
is a pause at the end of a majority of the lines,
while in the last three the line frequently runs
on, without any pause, into the next one in order to make complete sense. In the first group
you think of the line as the unit, but in the second the sentence and not the line is the unit.
Lines that pause at the end are "end-stopped";
those that do not pause are "run-on." Moreover, the regular ten-syllable line prevails in
the first three plays cited, while the eleven-
syllable line is very common in the second
three. The extra syllable may be a monosyllabic
word or the final syllable of a word of more
than one syllable (called a "feminine ending").
Monosyllables at the end of a line, such as
conjunctions, prepositions, and pronouns, are
called "weak" and "light" endings; they are
common in *The Winter's Tale, Cymbeline,* and
*The Tempest.* Scholars have generally agreed
that plays having chiefly end-stopped lines are
earlier and those with a great many run-on lines
are later; they also point out that weak and
light endings are far more numerous in later
plays.

The following passages from three typical
plays illustrate the foregoing statements and
should be carefully noted. The first selection is

from *A Midsummer Night's Dream*, the second from *As You Like It*, and the third from *The Tempest*:

> Having once this juice,
> I'll watch Titania while she is asleep,
> And drop the liquor of it in her eyes.
> The next thing then she waking looks upon,
> Be it on lion, bear, or wolf, or bull,
> On meddling monkey, or on busy ape,
> She shall pursue it with the soul of love;
> And ere I take this charm from off her sight,
> As I can take it with another herb,
> I'll make her render up her page to me.
>
> Act II, 1. Oberon's speech.

All these lines are perfectly regular, end-stopped lines. But such mechanical regularity is fortunately not carried throughout this or any other play.

> O good old man, how well in thee appears
> The constant service of the antique world,
> When service sweat for duty, not for meed!
> Thou art not for the fashion of these times,
> Where none will sweat but for promotion,
> And having that, do choke their service up
> Even with the having: it is not so with thee.
> But, poor old man, thou prun'st a rotten tree,

That cannot so much as a blossom yield
In lieu of all thy pains and husbandry.
But come thy ways; we'll go along together.

Act II, 3. Orlando's speech.

In these eleven lines three are run-on, and the
final line has a feminine ending. In the fourth
line it is necessary to pronounce "promotion"
as four syllables. The lines are less choppy than
in the first selection: the metrical characteristics are fairly typical of the middle period.
Here is a speech from a later, perhaps the latest,
play:

Admired Miranda!
Indeed the top of admiration! worth
What's dearest to the world! Full many a lady
I have eyed with best regard and many a time
The harmony of their tongues hath into bondage
Brought my too diligent ear: for several virtues
Have I liked several women; never any
With so full soul, but some defect in her
Did quarrel with the noblest grace she owed
And put it to the foil: but you. O you,
So perfect and so peerless, are created
Of every creature's best!

Act III, 1. Ferdinand's speech.

Nine of these twelve lines are run-on, and there
are six feminine endings. The movement is

quite free and the pauses varied; the verse approaches prose in its freedom. It is utterly devoid of artificiality. This is characteristic of the later plays.

It is particularly in the maturer plays of Shakespeare that we find many passages in which sense and sound unite to make a perfect harmony. Such is the effect of Hamlet's dying words to his friend Horatio:

If thou didst ever hold me in thy heart,
Absent thee from felicity awhile,
And in this harsh world draw thy breath in pain
To tell my story.

In the last two acts of *Antony and Cleopatra*, after the Roman general and the Egyptian queen have been defeated by Augustus Caesar, occur numerous lines reflecting in their subdued tempo the twilight atmosphere of a lost cause. This is felt in Antony's command to his friend Eros to take off his armor:

Unarm, Eros; the long day's task is done
And we must sleep.

And also in Cleopatra's order to Iras just before she applies the deadly asp to her breast:

Give me my robe, put on my crown; I have
Immortal longings in me: now no more
The juice of Egypt's grape shall moist this lip.

Perhaps the supreme example of majestic harmony in imagery and idea is found in Prospero's
speech to Ferdinand after the Masque of Ceres
has vanished:

Be cheerful, sir.
Our revels now are ended. These our actors,
As I foretold you, were all spirits and
Are melted into air, into thin air:
And, like the baseless fabric of this vision,
The cloud-capp'd towers, the gorgeous palaces,
The solemn temples, the great globe itself,
Yea, all which it inherit, shall dissolve
And, like this insubstantial pageant faded,
Leave not a rack behind. We are such stuff
As dreams are made on, and our little life
Is rounded with a sleep.

Relying on the various kinds of evidence just
discussed, critics have traced Shakespeare's development from about 1590 to about 1612 —
roughly speaking, twenty years of dramatic
activity. This development is based on the
assumption that an author undergoes marked
changes in mood and expression as he grows

older. Sensing these changes as reflected in the plays, critics have arranged them according to the several stages in a widening and deepening of mind and art. Though such an arrangement of the plays is perhaps more romantic than scientific, the division of them into four groups is convenient and has now become conventional.

In the first period, extending from about 1590 to 1595, Shakespeare was learning his art by an experimentation which probably involved the doing over of old plays. He consciously followed the rules of the game, had a regard for precedent, was somewhat imitative, and in general rather conservative. He was then, we may say, informally serving his dramatic apprenticeship.

In the second period, from about 1595 to 1600, he had gained in freedom of technique and expression. During these five or six years he wrote most of his historical plays and his happier comedies: the dramas of these years reflect his interest in three hundred years of English political history and also in the romance of high life. In the histories he exploits the royal way of life in court and camp, with its triumphs and defeats, its weaknesses and virtues. He follows the traditional lore of old chronicles in his painting of royal personages. In the comedy group he utilizes the popular romances of his own time and those of earlier days, transforming their crudely drawn characters into lovely English ladies and gallant gentlemen of wit and gaiety who talk brilliantly in verse and prose of beauty and distinction. Plays like *The Merchant of Venice*, *As You Like It*, *Twelfth Night*, and *Much Ado about Nothing* belong to what is called high comedy. It is in this second period that Shakespeare has attained mastery of his art.

The third period, from about 1600 to 1608, shows a marked change of tone. Leaving the wars and tumults of kings and the sunlit uplands of romance, he plunges into the depths of tragic gloom. He is now primarily concerned not with what men do but with the effects of their actions on themselves and others, the disastrous consequences of what they do. The dramatist turns his eyes inward and probes into the mysteries of human life entangled in the web of suffering and retribution. Revenge, ambition, jealousy, ingratitude, pride, and imperial passion are the great themes of these plays, which are psychological in their analytical revelation of character and motive. To this period belong the four supreme tragedies — *Hamlet*, *Macbeth*, *Othello*, and *King Lear*.

Here also belong *Antony and Cleopatra, Cori-olanus*, and the tragi-comedies, *Measure for Measure, All's Well That Ends Well*, and *Troi-lus and Cressida*.

In the fourth period, from about 1608 to 1612, the dramatist has ascended to the serene heights of pure romance. No longer is there any tense concern about the "problems" of life. The pangs of human passion are less acute in the remote regions of a humanized fairyland. Enchanted islands in far-off seas, distant strands for the salvage of shipwrecked infants, Bohemias with seacoasts, pastoral scenes for young lovers, and mountain caves for the rest of wandering princesses: this is the sort of setting one finds in these last plays. Legendary kings and courtiers alternate with very English shepherds, shepherdesses, and clowns. In the final act the long-lost wife or husband is restored, and the daughter, exposed years ago to the wild waves, is home again. Separation is followed by ultimate reunion, alienation by friendship, and transgression by forgiveness. "Pardon's the word to all," says King Cymbeline to the erring ones in the final scene. These romances — *Cymbeline, The Winter's Tale, The Tempest*, and the partly Shakespearean *Pericles* — are essentially dramatic poems celebrating peace and happiness after separation and suffering. They give an atmosphere of serenity to the concluding period of Shakespeare's literary life.

Though this division of the plays into four groups — apprenticeship, mastery, tragic gloom, and serenity — is somewhat arbitrary, it at least shows the general trend in Shakespeare's development as a dramatist. It serves to emphasize the predominant note in the early, the middle, and the later plays, as one compares them and attempts to classify them according to the several kinds of evidence. The following list of the plays is so arranged:

### EARLY

*Love's Labour's Lost, Comedy of Errors, Two Gentlemen of Verona, A Midsummer Night's Dream, Richard III,* 3 parts of *Henry VI* (possibly done over by Shakespeare as his earliest dramatic work), *Titus Andronicus.*

### MATURE

*Romeo and Juliet, Merchant of Venice, Taming of the Shrew, Merry Wives of Windsor, Much Ado about Nothing, As You Like It, Twelfth Night, Richard II, Henry IV* (1 and 2), *Henry V, Julius Caesar.*

## TRAGIC GLOOM

*Troilus and Cressida, All's Well That Ends Well, Measure for Measure* (dark and ironical comedies); *Hamlet, Othello, King Lear, Macbeth* (the four great tragedies); *Timon of Athens, Antony and Cleopatra.*

## SERENITY

*Cymbeline, The Winter's Tale, The Tempest.*

Because the composition dates of several of the plays are quite uncertain, it is difficult to classify them. *Romeo and Juliet*, for instance, is now regarded as later than formerly and is therefore excluded from the early group; *A Midsummer Night's Dream* may be put too early; *Julius Caesar* probably preceded *Hamlet* and is so classified. All this means that certain dramas are in a twilight zone, so to speak, in attempts to group the plays. Much of this classification is, of course, based on pure inference.

Modern costumes designed for *The Winter's Tale*.
Drawing by Albert Rutherston, 1928

# HOW THE PLAYS
## ARE CONSTRUCTED

THE five-act division of a Shakespearean play was a thousand-year-old inheritance from classical drama. The plays of ancient Rome had five acts. Shakespeare and his editors simply followed the traditional practice. The earliest English drama, known to us as Miracle and Morality plays, had no act divisions, but the Tudor dramatists adopted the structure of the Latin plays read in schools and universities. Indeed, the Elizabethan drama, as already pointed out, shows in various ways the influence of the classical. According to the traditional theory of dramatic art, the first act introduced the "exciting force" of the plot, the second act developed this by exposition, the third act brought the action to a crisis, or climax, the fourth act began the unraveling (dénouement) of the plot, and the fifth act brought about the catastrophe, or tragic conclusion. Theoretically, the first half of the play, up to the crisis, or climax, constituted the rising action (complication) and the other half the falling action (resolution). In general, this upward movement to a crisis, or turning point, followed by a downward movement to the final catastrophe, is found in Shakespearean tragedy, but not, of course, with such mechanical regularity as the theory implies. This dramatic technique will be made clearer by using two Shakespearean plays as illustrations.

The first act of *Romeo and Juliet*, for instance, reveals the feud between two families, Romeo's presence at his enemy's masked ball, and the fateful infatuation of the young lovers, which is the exciting, or impelling, force of the plot. The second act brings the moonlight meeting of the lovers and closes with their marriage. In the third act Romeo's kinsman Mercutio is fatally wounded by Tybalt, whom

Romeo promptly kills. For this deed he is banished from Verona; the parting of the lovers follows. The crisis, or climax, of the play has been reached. The fourth act is concerned with the thin minor plot — the plans for the marriage of Juliet with Paris — closing with the supposed death of Juliet. This is the beginning of the end in the fifth act which brings on the catastrophe: Romeo and Juliet are reunited in death. But, as often happens in a Shakespearean tragedy, there is light after the dark ending, in this case the reconciliation of the two long-hostile families.

Let us next consider in these respects the most symmetrical in structure of the great tragedies, *Macbeth*. The prediction of the witches and the determination of Macbeth to kill the king and get the throne form the exciting, or impelling, action. The murder of Duncan in the second act makes Macbeth king and also arouses fear and suspicion. Banquo is put out of the way by the new king's orders, but Macbeth, unable to control himself any longer, breaks down at the banquet in the third act. This is the crisis; and after this Macbeth is on the defensive against the forces closing in about him. In desperation he fights against fate with violent courage, but feels himself losing. The

fifth act brings swift retribution: Macduff and
Malcolm, who had fled to England, return;
Lady Macbeth gives way under nervous strain;
faced by his foes and wrought upon by the
startling fulfillment of prophecy, Macbeth dies
"with harness on his back" in the fight with
Macduff. The catastrophe is followed by the
announcement that King Malcolm is to be
crowned at Scotland's old capital of Scone.

Other Shakespearean tragedies show the crisis of the action in a less clear-cut fashion than
the two just discussed. In *Othello*, for instance,
the climax is psychological; it occurs in the
masterly third scene of the third act when
Othello, overcome in his mental wrestling
match with the villain Iago, is convinced of
Desdemona's unfaithfulness. In *Hamlet* the crisis is not so much in any action as it is in in-
action, namely, the failure of Hamlet to kill the
king when he has an opportunity as Claudius
is kneeling in the prayer scene (III, 3). After
that, Hamlet is on the defensive and the king
hot on the offensive. It is true, of course, that to
kill the king at such a moment would have
seemed too much like assassination. Moreover,
it would have ended the play prematurely. And
it was quite in character with Hamlet to hesitate, reflect on the matter, and do nothing. He

must wait for a more convenient season, which, one suspects, will turn out to be the catastrophe. At any rate, the lost chance means that the falling action has begun. In *Julius Caesar* the crisis is in the psychological effect of Antony's speech at Caesar's funeral upon the crowd which, fired with rage against the conspirators, turns on Caesar's enemies. Somewhere about the middle of a play, then, comes in one way or another the turning point of the plot.

Comedy is generally less formal in structure than tragedy. The exciting force and the crisis, or climax, may not be so evident or so definite in comedy. The happy ending, of course, takes the place of the tragic catastrophe. In the tragi-comedies, as the name implies, the serious, ominous action dominates the first half of the play, changing after a fairly well marked break to a happier tone. Most comedy, indeed, begins with an uncertain situation, proceeding through trouble and suspense to a fortunate ending; and the difference between comedy proper and tragi-comedy is largely one of degree in the serious action. The history plays, centering as they do about outstanding individuals, resemble in this respect the one-man tragedies. They differ, however, from both comedy and tragedy in being more episodic in movement. The historical plays are the only dramas of Shakespeare that form a series, and they are the only plays that have more than one "part." *Henry VI*, with its three parts, is a dramatized story of one man and his times; and *Henry IV*, with its two parts, is a ten-act drama of which the preceding *Richard II* is the prologue and *Henry V* the glorious epilogue. The three plays form a dramatic epic of patriotism ending in the triumph of Shakespeare's most heroic king. The exciting force in a history play is usually the desire for conquest or defense, and the crisis, or turning point, is either a battle or a revolt of the king's supporters. In general, structure in historical plays is simpler than in comedies and tragedies proper, for the historical order of events in the old chronicles is usually followed. The dramatist occasionally violates the proper sequence, however, selecting, relating, and changing his source materials as his artistic instinct dictates.

Illustrations of the foregoing statements about structure in comedies and histories may now be drawn from a few plays. In *As You Like It*, for instance, the exciting force is the banishment of certain persons to a forest, where love in romantic surroundings begins, continues, and happily ends. The crisis is in Act III, scene 2, with the meeting of Orlando and Rosalind, a rather mild incident but of great importance. *The Merchant of Venice* gets into action with the borrowing of a sum of money from a Jew by a merchant who gives his bond to pay it at a certain time. The crisis of the play occurs when Bassanio, the merchant's friend, chooses the right casket in Act III, scene 2, for on that choice will depend the salvation of the merchant. But the spectacular climax of the action is the trial scene in the fourth act. This great scene is also the tragic catastrophe for Shylock, ending the suspense and virtually terminating the action, for the short fifth act is a lyric of reunion in a moonlit atmosphere of relief.

The comedy of *Much Ado about Nothing* has its disturbing and complicating force in Don John's intrigue against Claudio, and its crisis, or climax, in the melodramatic interruption of the marriage in the church (Act IV, scene 1). One of the most marked illustrations of both exciting force and crisis in Shakespeare may be found in *The Winter's Tale*. A husband's violent jealousy of his wife early in the play leads to her supposed death in the third act and the banishment of her infant daughter. This tragic action is the perfect crisis of the drama. After an interval of sixteen years be-

tween the third and fourth acts — the longest
in Shakespeare — come restoration and general
reunion. The second half of the play, following
the break, is quite different from the first and
possible only in romance.

Two historical plays will serve to illustrate
impelling force and crisis in that type of drama.
Richard II, in the play of that name, arouses
opposition among his nobles and other subjects
by his arbitrary actions and his confiscation of
property. On his return from Ireland, from
which he has been recalled by rebellion at
home, he is captured by the followers of his
rival (Act III), brought to trial, and forced to
surrender his crown (Act IV). His capture is
the turning point. The exciting force in *Henry
V* is the royal desire to recapture lost lands in
France, for which purpose a military expedition invades that country. The crisis comes in
Act IV when the English king wins the great
battle of Agincourt. As these examples show,
the turning point in comedy and history sometimes occurs in the fourth act, while in tragedy it usually happens in the third act.

The structural elements just discussed are
fundamentally those of classical drama, which
strongly influenced the continental and English drama of the Renaissance. In this Greek

A memorial to "The Swan of Avon" in Trinity Church, Stratford-on-Avon. Shakespeare is buried here

and Roman heritage there was a clear distinction between tragedy and comedy: a tone of
high seriousness characterized the one and a
spirit of playfulness the other. The plays of
Seneca are consistently tragic and those of
Plautus consistently comic. But comedy by its
very nature had more freedom than tragedy,
for it reflected phases of contemporary life,
realistically and often satirically, while tragedy, on a higher plane, was stiff and stately in
its remoteness from the passing scene. The late
pre-Shakespearean plays show these inherited
dramatic traits: *Gorboduc*, for instance, which
closely follows its Senecan model, is an unrelieved tragedy of bloody revenge; and the early
comedy of *Ralph Roister Doister* is true in
structure and manner to its Roman prototypes,
the comedies of Plautus and Terence. In a classical play and in its imitative English product
there was little or no mixing of dramatic types:
each dramatic type followed its own traditions,
tragedy more rigidly and comedy more loosely.
And these traditions, particularly in tragedy,
had been formed into laws going back to Aristotle's formulation of practice in Greek drama.

It is different in the romantic drama of
Shakespeare and other Elizabethans. With the
exception of Ben Jonson, the Elizabethan play-

wrights disregarded the "rules" of the classical drama. Notable among these rules were those of the three dramatic "unities": the unity of time, limiting the action or story of the play to a period of twenty-four hours; the unity of place, confining the action to one locality; and the unity of plot, or subject, restricting the action to a single story. While Aristotle had positively advocated only the last unity, later critics adopted all three as dramatic law and gospel. Shakespeare violated all the unities except in one play, *The Tempest*, in which, as if to show the classicists what a romanticist could do, he observed all three. In two respects Shakespeare notably departed from traditional classical usage: (1) he sometimes put two stories, occasionally three, into a play, so fusing them as to give the reader or spectator an impression of oneness in the plot; and (2) he introduced various devices to give variety and lifelikeness to the action, such as masques, "dumb shows," playlets, gravedigging, pageants, songs, and clowning. In other words, he mixed tragedy and comedy. Knowing that life itself is a mixture of gloom and gladness, tears and laughter, the high and the low, virtue and villainy, he proceeded to hold the mirror up to human nature. That is romantic drama, which is free to light up the tragic with flashes of the comic, and to darken the comic with somber tints.

The double plot is found more often in Shakespearean comedy than in tragedy. An outstanding example is *The Merchant of Venice*, in which there are two longer stories, one shorter story, and an episode. The first story is that of the bond and pound of flesh; the second is that of the caskets and the beautiful heiress; the third is the Lorenzo-Jessica love affair; the incident of the rings is an entertaining episode to relieve the serious action. Two separate stories, which seem to have little connection, are skillfully fused into a greater unity which also includes two minor love affairs. This comedy is a tissue woven of several different strands.

*A Midsummer Night's Dream* is a bewildering complex of actions: the two sets of lovers and their confused identities, the intermeddling fairies and their fantastic doings, the "rude mechanicals" rehearsing and presenting a play, and the royal couple whose wedding is to be celebrated. In *Much Ado about Nothing* two stories are wrought into the plot: the love of Claudio and Hero and the association of Benedick and Beatrice, which, because of its witty dialogue, is more interesting to the modern reader than the Claudio-Hero part of the

play. With these two strands is interwoven another — the constable group who are irresist-
ibly funny because of their pretentious igno-
rance and blundering English. These three
strands — the serious, the ironical, and the
comic — are perfectly blended in this socially
brilliant comedy. These illustrations are suffi-
cient to warrant the assertion that Shakespearean comedy is a harmony of stories.

Only one of the four great tragedies is a
two-plot play, *King Lear*. The other three —
*Hamlet, Othello,* and *Macbeth* — have one central story, with occasional relief elements in
scene and character. In *King Lear*, however,
there are two plots so clearly defined and con-
tinuous that it would be more accurate to call
the secondary plot the parallel plot instead of
the subplot. The Lear story — an old man with
one good and two bad daughters — and the
Gloucester story — an old man with one good
and one bad son — run along from the first to
the fifth act, with many similarities of action
and motive. Lear is more sinned against than
sinning, and so is Gloucester; Lear is the victim
of his own poor judgment and credulity, and
so is Gloucester; and each is the object of filial
ingratitude. In no other tragedy of Shakespeare
is there such striking parallelism in plot and

persons as in *King Lear*. And yet Shakespeare put together in this play two tales which he got from different sources, weaving them into the larger unity of a colossal spiritual tragedy. This union of two or more distinct stories, related through eliminations and additions, is one of Shakespeare's most signal achievements in dramaturgy. And even more remarkable than this feat of construction is the re-creation of lifeless characters and the outright creation of others.

Mention has been made of the introduction of certain minor elements in the plays for variety and relief. One of these is the Masque, a spectacular performance of song and dance in which mythological characters take part. The finest example of this sort of entertainment in Shakespeare is the Masque of Ceres in the fourth act of *The Tempest*, an allegory of the fruitfulness of Nature, which was presumably acted at the betrothal or marriage of an English princess. Another diversion found in Shakespeare is the "dumb show" such as that in *Hamlet*, preceding and preparing for the play within the play; or the prophetic "apparitions" called up by the witches for Macbeth. Shakespeare's "fools," or clowns, are the greatest in the world's drama, delighting by their humorous philosophy of life, particularly Touchstone in *As You Like It* and the nameless Fool in *King Lear*. And with these should be mentioned that incomparable rogue Autolycus in *The Winter's Tale*. An important means of relief and atmospheric effect is the great variety of songs which are scattered through the plays. These lyrics afford breathing spells in the tense dramatic action; they serve to entertain the audience while necessary stage adjustments are being made; and they color the scene with a tone of weirdness or pastoral beauty or exultant joyousness or somber suggestion. The metrical contrast between these lyrical measures and the prevailing blank verse and frequent rhyming couplets is itself a welcome relief to hearer and reader. These varied elements in the make-up of Shakespearean drama give it a widespread appeal which is lacking in the rigid unity of the classical.

An early printing plant as represented by Stradanus,
Antwerp, about 1600

# HOW TO READ SHAKESPEARE

THE right understanding of a Shakespearean play will depend upon the reader's
temperament, general culture, and knowledge
of Elizabethan dramatic conditions. Readers of
the great dramatist, including literary critics,
in every succeeding age have interpreted
him with varying degrees of emphasis, or difference, as they have been influenced by personal preferences, contemporary taste, and acquaintance with Shakespeare's own time. The

late seventeenth century, and much of the eighteenth, viewed him as a great but irregular genius who, because he violated the "rules" of classic art, needed to be brought into line with current ideas of dramatic technique. That he was original these critics admitted; he was faithful to human nature, yes — rather too faithful. It would, they thought, have been better if he had been more "proper," less exuberant, more restrained. Critics of the late eighteenth century and early nineteenth, notably Samuel Taylor Coleridge, thought of Shakespeare as a poet and philosopher who wrote plays, seeing him through their own eyes in an essentially romantic age much given to philosophizing. The aim of this kind of criticism was an appreciation of the beautiful, the exaltation of Shakespeare as an interpreter of life by his wise and witty reflections or comments on men and manners. Critics as well as readers were much impressed with the beauty and the wisdom to be found in his plays. Volumes of "purple" passages from Shakespeare were published for those who wished to read "the best in Shakespeare," while Charles and Mary Lamb's *Tales from Shakespeare* acquainted juvenile readers with the stories of such plays as might properly be told to early Victorian youth. This

idealistic and moralistic conception of Shakespeare prevailed during much of the nineteenth
century.

But Shakespeare is more than a poet and philosopher. He is, above all, a maker of plays.
That fact is a rediscovery of twentieth-century
criticism after the aesthetic and moral over-
emphasis of the last century. The historical approach to Shakespeare has brought about a
more realistic attitude toward the plays, growing out of attempts to restore, as far as possible,
the conditions under which they were written
and first produced. Modern scholarship, as
Professor Kittredge has remarked, seeks to find
out what Shakespeare actually said and what
he meant at the time of saying it; and such
knowledge cannot be attained by detaching the
dramatist from his contemporary background.
Shakespeare was of his age; he thought and
wrote as a man of the English Renaissance.

There are numerous customs or usages in his
plays which are common to the Elizabethan
drama in general, though foreign to modern
usage, and these customs seem natural only in
the light of our knowledge of the stagecraft of
that day. The soliloquy and the aside, for example, have almost disappeared from modern
drama, but they seem perfectly proper in a

Shakespearean play when one realizes that the actor was so near the spectators on three sides of the projecting stage in an Elizabethan theatre as to be on intimate terms with them. He might impart information to these close neighbors either by way of explanation or as a revelation of his own inmost thoughts. Moreover, the soliloquy and the aside, one suspects, are sometimes the spoken opinions of Shakespeare himself. The declamatory speech, so out of place in a conversational play of today, was liked by an Elizabethan audience, who gloried in rhetorical display even when it was "full of sound and fury, signifying nothing." These outmoded characteristics of Shakespearean drama seemed quite natural to sixteenth- and seventeenth-century audiences. And so, for that matter, did dialogue in verse, which to our practical age is highly unnatural, though we still applaud the language, manner, and dress of grand opera. Verse was a normal form of dramatic speech in Shakespeare's time.

Between reading a play and seeing it there is, of course, a wide difference, but the more clearly we visualize it in action the more surely we may understand it. A Shakespearean play is a dramatized story originally seen and heard on the stage. The narrative and the characters make the moving drama. It is not merely a series of inwoven pictures like a tapestry, but a succession of dynamic scenes from life. And properly to read a play is to visualize it in the imagination, to identify it with reality even though the thing should be the wildest melodrama. The average uncritical listener to a Shakespearean play hardly thinks of it as poetry. He probably thinks little about the medium of expression; to him it is a good or poor show in proportion to its ability or inability to hold his attention. He is not likely to condemn Hamlet's inability to act or to become emotional about the beauty and depth of his speeches, some of which seem to him to be made up of familiar quotations, anyhow! The Prince of Denmark's caution and delay appear natural, for killing a king is a ticklish business, requiring roundabout methods. That Hamlet pauses at intervals to talk the matter over with himself is natural. In doing so the young Prince incidentally makes some wise comments on life and death. But it is neither the profundity of his philosophy nor the poetic quality of his language that enthralls the man in the pit (our top gallery) and a good many of those in better positions. What the average spectator is mainly interested in is the story of how a young man tries to catch the murderer of his father and finally succeeds, though at the loss of his own life. This exciting game — the ghost business, the mousetrap play, Ophelia's drowning, the pirates, the grave-digging, and the fencing match — are simply entertaining episodes. "The play's the thing to catch the conscience of the king," as Hamlet said, and it is also the thing to catch and hold the attention of the reader.

The conception of a play as a dramatized story to be seen and heard in a theatre is neces-sary to the full enjoyment of it. This rather obvious statement needs emphasizing today when the study of Shakespeare in educational institutions may lead young men and women to think of the plays, elaborately annotated and introduced, as having been written for class use. Well, Shakespeare didn't know he was a classic any more than the ancients knew they be-longed to antiquity. He never thought of his plays as unhappy hunting grounds for linguis-tic puzzles and subtle symbolism. Of course, we may, and probably do, get out of them more than the dramatist consciously put into them, but that is true of all great literature, particu-larly poetry. The suggestiveness of many lines may invite more than one interpretation of them, to say nothing of corrupt texts. One must, however, guard against reading into them meanings or inferences which the circumstances or connection may not warrant. It is true that certain words in Shakespeare have a different meaning today. In the following speech of Polonius to Laertes (*Hamlet*, I, 3), for instance, several words have changed in meaning:

And these few precepts in thy memory
See thou character. Give thy thoughts no tongue,
Nor any unproportioned thought his act.
Be thou familiar, but by no means vulgar. . . .
Give every man thy ear, but few thy voice;
Take each man's censure, but reserve thy judg-
ment.

*Character* means *engrave*, and is accented on the second syllable; *his* is *its* in modern English; *vulgar* is *free and easy*, or *extremely familiar;* and *censure* is simply *opinion*, without any idea of blame. The more common of the hundred or so words in Shakespeare with older meanings may soon be learned from a glossary. Elizabethan English, after all, is not very different from modern. It is not so much the language of Shakespeare that may hinder one's enjoyment of a play as it is failure to visualize the action on a stage.

There may, of course, be literary enjoyment of a play without an understanding of its purely dramatic, or acting, qualities. Most readers of Shakespeare today think of him as the great poet, the master of character portrayal. To them his works are standard literature, quite indispensable to the libraries of men and women who are cultured or who would like to be thought so. Those who actually read the plays find great pleasure in the glorious poetry and moral satisfaction at Shakespeare's insight into human personality. They are keenly interested in the motivation of his characters, high and low, clowns and kings, villains and lovers; they are thrilled by his masterful manipulation of men and events in critical situations. These closet readers of Shakespeare, who perhaps never saw a play in action, may know him better and quote him with greater gusto than your specialist in the art of acting and Elizabethan dramaturgy. Indeed, the intelligent reader, and sometimes even the accomplished Shakespearean scholar, may so greatly prefer his own interpretation of the dramatist that he will not go to see a play butchered on the stage. He would rather see it in imagination, looking not with the eyes but with the mind. Such an attitude is quite understandable; there is so much in a

Shakespearean play to be remembered and thought on that reading it in the quiet of the study may be preferable to seeing it in the garish social and professional atmosphere of the theatre. The actor, most likely, is unable to "speak trippingly on the tongue"; he mouths his words, has no sensitiveness to poetic inflection, and in general mutilates the beauty of the lines by a slovenly or raucous rendering. For the poetry of Shakespeare, whether blank verse or lyric, is so much a part of his greatness that no vocal interpretation is adequate without an audible awareness of the rhythm. And in the silence of the library the sensitive reader may inwardly discern the lilt in many a Shakespearean verse.

Reading aloud is helpful to an appreciation of Shakespeare's verse as well as to an understanding of the action, setting, and characters. Ideally, dramatic verse is spoken poetry, just as lyric verse is the poetry of song, and both are at their best when spoken. Certainly the oral interpretation of a play, whether in verse or prose, is a sure way of dramatizing it to the imagination in sound and sense. Older readers of Shakespeare used to memorize many passages from the plays, which they loved to declaim to appreciative listeners. A well-known

banker in a certain Southern city, meeting me
on a street corner, would hold me with his
glittering eye while he poured forth lengthy
passages from the dramatist. Walt Whitman
shouted speeches from *King Lear* to the rhythm
of the surging sea off the Long Island coast.
These lovers of the actor-poet found aesthetic
and moral delight in *hearing* him. Some of them
were, no doubt, ignorant of many fine points
about the plays, but they succeeded in vitaliz-
ing them as few cloistered scholars do. We
know a great deal *about* Shakespeare today, but
it is possible, what with outlines and other
"helps," that we may see him only through a
glass darkly. Reading Shakespeare aloud may
be the beginning of a personal acquaintance
which may ripen into friendship.

But reading Shakespeare aloud is not necessarily a declamatory proceeding. The old-fash-
ioned Shakespearean actor was far more given
to oratorical display than the modern, just as
the older American public speaker impressed
his audience by a booming delivery and many
gestures. That overdone style of speaking now
seems unnatural. Even in Shakespeare's day, if
we may trust Hamlet's instructions to the players, oratorical violence made "the unskillful
laugh and the judicious grieve." There are, to

A scene from *The Two Gentlemen of Verona* as painted
by a nineteenth-century artist, Holman Hunt

Macbeth is appalled at seeing Banquo's ghost. From Or-
son Welles' Mercury Theatre production of *Macbeth*

be sure, formal speeches in Shakespeare which may be declaimed with good effect, but for the most part a restrained emotional intensity is more effective. Descriptive passages in the plays, of which there are many in place of stage scenery, should certainly not be declaimed. And soliloquies, those speeches in which the character is thinking aloud, should be rendered in a conversational, though not monotonous, tone. Vocal interpretation of Shakespeare is most successful when it is in harmony with the thought and the occasion. In the interpretation of Shakespeare's verse, tonal modulation and facial expression are both essential. Mannerisms are to be studiously avoided lest the reader unconsciously convert the dramatic into the melodramatic. In general, naturalness of speech and manner is the prime requisite.

Those who heard the great American actor Edwin Booth give Hamlet's "To be or not to be" soliloquy recall how quietly it was done. Sitting in a chair he talked without gesture, quietly, almost meditatively, oblivious of Ophelia's presence in the room. He was not speaking to anybody in particular, but just uttering his own thoughts on an old and absorbing question with which his recent experiences had brought him face to face. He was making no speech — only

debating with himself whether, under the circumstances, it was better to

> bear those ills we have
> Than fly to others that we know not of.

Quite different in tone is the address of
Henry V urging on his soldiers at the siege of
Harfleur (*Henry V*, III, 1):

> Once more unto the breach, dear friends,
>                    once more,
> Or close the wall up with our English dead!
> In peace there's nothing so becomes a man
> As modest stillness and humility;
> But when the blast of war blows in our ears,
> Then imitate the action of the tiger:
> Stiffen the sinews, summon up the blood,
> Disguise fair nature with hard-favored rage.

Such a speech naturally invites a spirited rendering by the reader. But not so with occasional
speeches of a different type. The addresses of
Brutus and Antony at Caesar's funeral, for instance, are more varied in tone. Brutus's speech,
which is in prose, is addressed to the minds of
his hearers; it is a careful piece of logical reasoning. Antony's, which is in verse, is a piece
of persuasive oratory, beginning quietly, even

deferentially, gaining in momentum as the crowd emotionally responds, and reaching a final crescendo of mob appeal. A master of mob psychology, Antony arouses sympathy by revealing the people's debt to the dead dictator, passing from veiled irony to overt denunciation of his murderers. The expressive reading of this masterful speech demands an intonation varying in tempo and intensity from cool reasoning to a climactic emotional fervor.

For subdued emotional effect, with pathetic suggestion, there is no better example in Shakespeare than old Lear's speech to Cordelia (*King Lear*, V, 3):

> Come, let's away to prison;
> We two alone will sing like birds i' the cage.
> When thou dost ask me blessing, I'll kneel down
> And ask of thee forgiveness. So we'll live,
> And pray, and sing, and tell old tales, and laugh
> At gilded butterflies.

The old man, driven to insanity by the unfilial treatment of Goneril and Regan, has at last been rescued by Cordelia, but along with her he has been sent to prison. In her company, retired from the world, he longs for a peace which the reader knows is the false hope of age and weakness.

A fine illustration of restrained emotion touched with a fatalistic note and culminating in a tragic climax is found in Othello's last speech. Fully realizing that he has murdered an innocent woman and that he has nothing to live for now, Othello asks the officers who have arrested him to tell the whole truth about him and his deed when they return to Venice:

> Then must you speak
> Of one that loved not wisely but too well;
> Of one not easily jealous, but, being wrought,
> Perplexed in the extreme; of one whose hand,
> Like the base Indian, threw a pearl away
> Richer than all his tribe; of one whose sub-
>     dued eyes,
> Albeit unused to the melting mood,
> Drop tears as fast as the Arabian trees
> Their medicinal gum.

Then, after mentioning almost incidentally how he once killed a man who had slandered the Venetian state, Othello quite unexpectedly stabs himself. The reading aloud of this tense scene should show deep feeling without declamatory effect.

Two more well-known speeches in the plays, very different from those already cited, may be referred to here. The familiar lines in *As*

*You Like It*, beginning "All the world's a stage," are sometimes read as if they formed an oration. But they are really simply thoughtful or philosophical, as uttered by the melancholy Jaques. They explain the preceding remark by Duke Senior

> That this wide and universal theatre
> Presents more woful pageants than the scene
> Wherein we play in.

One of the most charming scenes in Shakespeare is the dialogue between the Duke and Viola (*Twelfth Night*, II, 4) in which the disguised Viola archly confesses her love to the unsuspecting Duke in language which has one meaning for him and another for the reader or audience:

*Viola.*   My father had a daughter loved a man,
              As it might be, perhaps, were I a woman,
              I should your lordship.
*Duke.*                         And what's her history?
*Viola.*   A blank, my lord. She never told her love,
              But let concealment, like a worm i' the
                                                    bud,
              Feed on her damask cheek; she pined in
                                                    thought,
              And with a green and yellow melancholy
              She sat like Patience on a monument,

> Smiling at grief. Was not this love in-
>                            deed? . . .
> *Duke.* But died thy sister of her love, my boy?
> *Viola.* I am all the daughters of my father's
>                            house,
>            And all the brothers too; — and yet I
>                            know not.

Obviously these speeches of Viola should be
spoken in a conversational tone of double suggestiveness. When one remembers that on the
public Elizabethan stage Viola was a boy actor
playing a woman's part but disguised as a page,
it is evident how difficult such an impersona-
tion was. The effective reading aloud of the
part is not an easy accomplishment.

In reading Shakespeare, then, the eye and the
ear should co-operate. Even when the reading
is silent the tone should be imaginatively heard.
For the study of the dramatist should be a vital
experience, and this can be completely achieved
only when the action of a play is visualized and
the speeches heard. Shakespeare did not, like
Browning, write closet dramas, but plays to be
seen and spoken. And even when his lines are
pure poetry, and not essentially dramatic, their
beauty is enhanced if read aloud. It is Shakespeare's glory to have combined poetic excellence with practical dramatic effectiveness.

The Tower of London. An engraving from J. Stow's
*Survey of London and Westminster*, 1598

## THE NONDRAMATIC POET

BESIDES the plays and the lyrics in them,
Shakespeare wrote several narrative poems
and many sonnets. Most of this was early work,
falling within the last decade of the sixteenth
century. *Venus and Adonis*, a long narrative
poem in six-line stanzas, was published in 1593.
It was dedicated to the popular young nobleman, Henry Wriothesley (generally pronounced Risley), Earl of Southampton, with
the usual exaggerated compliments of the day.
In his dedication Shakespeare speaks of the
poem as "the first heir of my invention" and
promises to honor his patron with "some graver

labour." This graver labor was realized the next year (1594) by the publication of *Lucrece* (generally called *The Rape of Lucrece*), a narrative poem in seven-line, or "rhyme royal," stanzas, dedicated to the same nobleman. Both poems were popular, ten editions of *Venus* appearing before Shakespeare's death and five of *Lucrece*. While Shakespeare had certainly done some dramatic writing before *Venus* and *Lucrece*, these were the first of his works to be published, and the only productions to which he ever wrote dedications. Moreover, these two poems, so far as we know, are the only products of his genius which Shakespeare authorized to be printed.

The source of *Venus and Adonis* is Ovid's *Metamorphoses*, which Shakespeare may have read at school. It is the story, quite familiar in the Renaissance, of how Venus wooed Adonis in vain; for she could not by the allurements of love persuade him to give up the chase of the wild boar, which, as Venus had feared, resulted in the youth's death. The myth is told by Shakespeare with certain variations from the original and with much description of nature, decorative effects liked by the Elizabethans and liberally employed by the poets. The vividness of many descriptive passages in the poem makes one feel that Shakespeare was drawing directly on the familiar scenery of his native Warwickshire. This stanza, for instance, seems suggested by an English sunrise:

Lo, here the gentle lark, weary of rest,
From his moist cabinet mounts up on high,
And wakes the morning, from whose silver breast
The sun arises in his majesty;
Who doth the world so gloriously behold
That cedar-tops and hills seem burnished gold.

And these lines on the hare chased by hounds might reflect personal experience:

Sometime he runs among a flock of sheep,
To make the cunning hounds mistake their smell,
And sometime where earth-delving conies keep,
To stop the loud pursuers in their yell.

Throughout the poem there is much conventional Renaissance coloring in figures of speech and epithets drawn from the stock material of an inherited poetical storehouse. Other contemporary poets, such as Marlowe, Lodge, and Spenser, also freely used this legendary matter in narrative verse. The sensuous imagery of Shakespeare's poem made a strong appeal: "The younger sort," wrote Gabriel Harvey in

1598, "takes much delight in Shakespeare's *Venus and Adonis.*"

For his other early poem, *Lucrece,* Shakespeare was indebted to Ovid's *Fasti* and Livy's *Histories* as sources, either directly or indirectly. The old story of how Lucretia, the chaste wife of a Roman general, was assaulted by King Tarquin's son Sextus, killed herself, and was avenged by her husband and the people of Rome, who banished the Tarquins forever, was a favorite with the older English poets. Chaucer had used it in his *Legend of Good Women* and Samuel Daniel in his *Complaint of Rosamond* (1592). *Lucrece,* like its predecessor, was also popular, but with a different set of readers. Gabriel Harvey thought that *Lucrece* was certain "to please the wiser sort." Indeed, the poem was greeted with a chorus of praise from critics and poets. It was hailed as a moral lesson on womanly chastity and was commended by a fellow of Cambridge University as "all-praise-worthy." The intensely human and tragic character of Lucrece makes it something of a drama, to say nothing of its political and patriotic quality as sealing the doom of Roman monarchy and foreshadowing the republic. There are dramatic situations: the stealthy tread of Tarquin and the opening of the doors, the dialogue between the ravisher and the victim, the letter from Lucrece to her husband, his arrival, her call for vengeance, and her suicide. The Renaissance love of decoration in descriptive scenes is here, of course; and the long examination by poor Lucrece of the painting of Troy, with Helen and Hecuba as sufferers from violence, was a tapestried speech dear to the Elizabethans. In writing his *Lucrece*, Shakespeare showed the feeling and the grasp which were later to reach perfection in his great tragedies.

Three poems attributed to Shakespeare for one reason or another are *A Lover's Complaint*, *The Passionate Pilgrim*, and *The Phoenix and the Turtle*. The first was included in Shakespeare's *Sonnets* published by Thorpe, the second in a tiny volume issued by the well-known printer Jaggard as by "W. Shakespeare," and the third in Robert Chester's anthology of contemporary verse. The *Complaint* is the lament of a deserted lady (the lover) to "a reverend man" (shepherd); the *Pilgrim* (lover) is another variation on the Venus-Adonis theme. *The Phoenix and the Turtle* (turtledove) is an allegorical poem, so difficult that few people today can understand it. *The Phoenix and the Turtle* seems to have been written by Shake-

# THE

# WORKS

## OF

Mr. *William Shakespear*;

### IN

## SIX VOLUMES.

---

ADORN'D with CUTS.

---

Revis'd and Corrected, with an Account of
the Life and Writings of the Author.

By *N. ROWE*, Esq;

---

## LONDON:

Printed for *Jacob Tonson*, within *Grays-Inn*
Gate, next *Grays-Inn* Lane. MDCCIX.

The title page of the first illustrated edition of Shakespeare's plays, edited by Nicholas Rowe, 1709

speare, perhaps in a whimsical or satirical mood. The *Complaint* and the *Pilgrim* are very doubtfully his, though they are generally included in "complete" editions of Shakespeare's works. Far more important than all these nondramatic poems, genuine and doubtful, are Shakespeare's sonnets, which Francis Meres in 1598 referred to as "his sugred Sonnets among his private friends."

This reference by Meres, the first mention of the *Sonnets* by a contemporary, implies that such was a common practice by Elizabethan poets. The author of short poems often allowed his literary friends to read them in his notebook and even to copy such verses as they particularly liked. Thus the original manuscript, as well as copies of part or all of it, might circulate from hand to hand. The poems would in this way have a fairly wide reading among a limited set of persons interested in the new poetry. There might be no intention of publication by the author; he wrote and passed his verses around for his own satisfaction and the delight of his friends. Later they might be collected and published, with or without the author's consent. Through some such process the sonnets of Shakespeare seem to have passed. At any rate, in 1609 one Thomas Thorpe, a London publisher, had a collection of Shakespeare's sonnets printed for the first time.

Thorpe dedicated the small volume *"To the onlie begetter of these insuing Sonnets Mr. W. H. all happinesse and that eternitie promised by our ever-living poet"*; and in so doing raised a question or two which may never be answered. Who was "Mr. W. H." and what does "begetter" mean? Various guesses have been made by scholars as to the identity of "Mr. W. H.," to whom the volume was dedicated. The two men most frequently mentioned have been Henry Wriothesley, Earl of Southampton, and William Herbert, Earl of Pembroke. It would be necessary, to be sure, to reverse the initials of the first if he is to be accepted as the inspirer of the sonnets, to say nothing of the impropriety of calling an English earl "mister." William Herbert perfectly fits the initials, but he also had a noble title. Moreover, Herbert, born in 1580, would have been rather young for the "friend" of the sonnets if they were written in the nineties. If "begetter" means the person who inspired the sonnets, as seems more reasonable, he might well have been a noble friend of Shakespeare; but if "begetter," as is possible, means the person who got the manuscript copy of the sonnets for the

publisher, then "Mr. W. H." may have been
some printer or other agent of Thorpe, or more
probably some gentleman of the time who had
read the manuscript. That the publisher should
have dedicated his volume to the man who pro-
cured the copy for him seems the less plausible
of the two theories, unless indeed the inspirer
and the getter were the same person. Whatever
the truth may be, it is certain that, thanks
to Thomas Thorpe, we have the *Sonnets* of
Shakespeare. Before discussing the poems themselves, something should be said about the sonnet in general.

The sonnet is primarily a continental Euro-
pean product which came from Italy to England in the sixteenth century. English courtiers,
notably Sir Thomas Wyatt and Henry Howard, Earl of Surrey, visited Italy, caught the
lyric fever raging there, and brought home the
germs which speedily infected English versi-
fiers. Much of the verse of Wyatt and Surrey,
along with that of others, was collected in a
popular anthology known as *Tottel's Miscel-
lany*, published by Richard Tottel in 1557. But
the sonnet is much older than that, going back
to the thirteenth century and Dante. The real
father of the sonnet, however, is fourteenth-
century Petrarch, who made the species fa-

mous in his romantic series of sonnets to Laura, the lovely lady with whom his name is forever linked. The sonnets of this Italian poet and his followers set the fashion of the English sonnets, which also owe something to the French sonnets of Desportes, Ronsard, and others. Wyatt followed the Italian form, consisting of fourteen lines divided into eight (the octave) and six (the sestet) and rhyming *abbaabbacdcdcd* (the sestet greatly varied). But Surrey changed the rhyme scheme into what later came to be known as the Elizabethan sonnet, used by Shakespeare: *ababcdcdefefgg,* that is, fourteen lines in iambic pentameter (five stresses), twelve in alternate rhyme, and a concluding couplet.

While the Elizabethan sonnet departed from the Italian in rhyme arrangement, it followed the Italian fairly closely in content and style. Noteworthy among the importations from Italian and French sonnets by English sonneteers were many conventional phrases and epithets, particularly those relating to the lady celebrated in the poems. She had luminous, devastating eyes, milk-white skin, and sweet breath; her extraordinary beauty, her chastity, and her angelic remoteness inspired a devotion almost hopeless in its chances of successful wooing.

The "cruel fair," whose flinty heart was in strange contrast to her gentle nature, was repeatedly assured of immortality through her lover's verse, which would, she was told, also immortalize the writer. The poet harped on the transient nature of physical beauty, his own unworthiness, his tearful experience in vainly trying to wear down the stony indifference of his lady, and on the autumnal signs of his wintry age. All these and other sentimental complaints, expressed in a complicated style abounding in similes and metaphors, were inherited by Elizabethan poets as traditional elements of the sonnet.

In the last two decades of the sixteenth century a perfect epidemic of sonneteering broke out among English poets, high and low. Sonnet writing became a literary vogue. Over two thousand sonnets were printed and many more were written, only to remain in manuscript and ultimately to perish. Some of these sonnets, strung together in loose sequences, were nothing more than exercises in a fashionable literary game; others were more or less autobiographical, telling erratically the story of a personal experience. Sir Philip Sidney wrote over a hundred sonnets on his love for Penelope Devereux, daughter of the first Earl of Essex, published after his death as *Astrophel and Stella*. Edmund Spenser composed a series which he named *Amoretti* ("love poems"), in many of which are set forth, figuratively, fragmentary aspects of his own life and love. Samuel Daniel, an eminent poet in his day, wrote sonnets to a lady he called Delia, and Michael Drayton, from Shakespeare's own Warwickshire, addressed his sequence to Idea, who sounds more abstract than real. Numerous romantic names were borrowed or invented by the sonneteers for their ladies, real or imaginary. Of all the cycles of sonnets that have come down to us three are outstanding for the beauty of their verse — Sidney's, Spenser's, and Shakespeare's.

The *Sonnets* of Shakespeare imply rather than definitely tell a story. The friend to whom most of them are addressed has stolen the love of the poet's mistress, but is forgiven by the poet, who loves his friend more than the "lost lady" who has played the poet false. Besides the "dark lady" involved in this triangular affair, there is a certain "rival poet" who has been praising Shakespeare's friend. Nobody knows who the brunette was or what contemporary poet is referred to. All we can infer about the identity of the friend is that he is a young man of high birth, accomplished and handsome. Such friendships between men were not uncommon among the Elizabethans. Classic examples in other nations will be recalled — Achilles and Patroclus, Damon and Pythias, David and Jonathan ("thy love to me was wonderful, passing the love of women"); and in Shakespeare's own plays, Hamlet and Horatio, and the two gentlemen of Verona. The first seventeen sonnets urge the friend to marry so that he may have children in whom his image will be perpetuated. There follows a long stretch of meditations and reflections: the friend's unfaithfulness, the poet's forgiveness and his undying love for this gifted youth, mention of certain absences (presumably on professional acting tours), comments on friendship, life, and destiny. The poet repeatedly assures his friend (as other sonnet writers do their ladies) that both will be immortalized in this verse. Most of the great Shakespearean sonnets come between XVIII and CXXVI; the remaining, concerned with the "dark lady" and other matters, have been likened by one critic to "a disordered appendix" which is painfully superfluous. The entire sonnet series is almost summed up in these lines from *Sonnet CXLIV:*

Two loves I have of comfort and despair,
Which like two spirits do suggest me still;
    [tempt me ever]
The better angel is a man right fair,
The worser spirit a woman colored ill.

There is a kind of unity in the *Sonnets*, but
certainly not an organic one. There are brief
successions of poems on closely related subjects, followed by others apparently irrelevant.
One gets the impression that they were written at various times over a number of years.
They might have been little poetic epistles addressed in the main to one friend. There is, of
course, no assurance that they are arranged
either chronologically or in the order of importance. Numerous attempts at rearrangement have not been convincing. And unless
some contemporary proof turns up, which is
not very likely, the *Sonnets* must be judged by
internal evidence, both as to order and content,
as they appear in Thorpe's collection. The
probability, however, is that some "knowing"
person got them for the publisher and decided
the order. As to the date of composition it may
be assumed that, as part of the Elizabethan sonneteering movement, most of them must have
been written in the last decade of the century.

But it is quite possible that some were written in the first years of the new century, and if so, among these would be the much-discussed *Sonnet CVII*, which has been interpreted as referring to Queen Elizabeth's death (1603).

With every reader of Shakespeare's sonnets the inevitable question arises: Are they autobiographical, or are they more or less conventional productions in which the sentiments revealed or suggested are imaginary? Did Shakespeare lay bare his heart in these poems which seem so personal, or did he, like other Elizabethan sonneteers, only dramatize in lyric form his poetic fancy? Might not a man in whom the dramatic instinct never slept, with whom playmaking and acting were normal activities, have naturally expressed himself dramatically in a series of sonnets also? Much may be said for this view, but perhaps more for the other. Unfortunately we know little about Shakespeare's inner life, except as it may be indirectly revealed in his plays; we have no personal facts to help us in an interpretation of his sonnets as we have in Sidney's and Spenser's. But after all, poetry is not factually true, lyric poetry least of all, for it is life seen through a temperament. The reader hardly expects absolute truth either

in a friend's or a lover's tributes, and it is the
poet's privilege to give to airy nothings a considerable degree of plausibility. As it has been
remarked by more than one critic, the writer
of a sonnet must *seem* to be telling the truth;
however at variance with fact such a poem may
be, it must appear to be sincere. Shakespeare's
sonnets sound so; and if, with a full knowledge
of the nature of the Elizabethan sonnet, one
must choose between the conventional and the
personal interpretation of his sonnets, one may
well take them at their face value. It is hard to
think that many of these feeling lines had no
personal significance, that what Shakespeare
wrote was nothing but a figment of his fancy.

His sonnets differ in several important respects from those making up other sequences.
Many of them celebrate the friendship (the
Elizabethans called it "love") of a man for a
man, not of a man for a woman, as was usual.
They have no poetic title; the woman who is
mentioned is criticized, not praised; far from
having a romantic name, she has no name at all.
She is certainly no heroine, but a charmer with
no strong claim to beauty. In one sonnet the
poet seems to be satirizing the typical Elizabethan lady-worship of the dabbler in verse:

My mistress' eyes are nothing like the sun;
Coral is far more red than her lips' red;
If snow be white, why then her breasts are dun;
If hairs be wires, black wires grow on her head.
I have seen roses damasked, red and white,
But no such roses see I in her cheeks.

And he concludes that his mistress "when she walks treads on the ground." Nothing could be farther from the Delias and Dianas and Licias of the sonneteers. Though departing in many respects from the conventional phrasing of the sonnet writers, Shakespeare does follow them in several particulars. He laments the swift passing of beauty, stresses the importance of posterity in which it may live again, exaggerates the age of the lover, plays on names (irresistible delight of the Elizabethans!), reiterates the lasting power of verse, and moderately loves "conceits." In these respects he was the child of his age, and no one can properly understand the sonnets without some knowledge of this relationship.

Fortunately, however, the enjoyment of the sonnets as poetry does not depend on a full knowledge of the matters just discussed. One does not have to solve the puzzles of dedication, date of composition, proper sequence, the

Puck, the mischievous fairy in *A Midsummer Night's Dream,* says, "Lord, what fools these mortals be!"

identities of the three persons involved, to ap-
preciate these poems as literature. We shall
never definitely know whether they are autobiographical fragments or only dramatic creations having an astonishing appearance of truth.
The poet may have gone through some such
experiences as those sketched in the sonnets,
or the vague and shadowy narrative may be
merely such stuff as dreams are made of. The
sonnets are hardly worth reading just for the
story; it is not a very pleasant one and leaves
something of a bad taste in the mouth. Taken
as a whole the sonnets are not as rewarding as
when read in parts. That is true of all sonnet
cycles and, indeed, of all lyrical series. A physical chain may not be stronger than its weakest
link, but a poetical chain is judged by its strongest links. In this Shakespearean sequence it is the
individual sonnet which counts most and not
the loosely joined succession.

The sonnets of Shakespeare contain some of
the greatest lyric verse in English poetry, verse
of such depth and beauty that it has captivated
successive generations of sensitive readers. Regardless of their immediate connection or original significance, whole sonnets and scores of
single lines have become the spiritual possession of the English-speaking peoples. This can

be said of no other sonnet sequence in our literature, and it may be truthfully said of only a fraction of the Shakespearean sonnets. One may remember, thanks to the anthologies, a sonnet of Daniel ("Care-charmer Sleep, son of the sable night"), one of Drayton ("Since there's no help, come let us kiss and part"), one or two of Sidney ("With how sad steps, O Moon, thou climbst the skies" and "Come, Sleep! O Sleep, the certain knot of peace"), and perhaps one or more of Spenser ("Like as a ship, that through the Ocean wide" and "Men call you fair and you do credit it"). One may recall a handful of sonnets from other Elizabethans, but (thanks also in part to the anthologies) a dozen or so from Shakespeare will come to mind without much effort.

Though early praised for their "sugared sweetness," the *Sonnets* of Shakespeare were late in receiving the full recognition for the high poetic merit which is accorded them today. Greater interest in the plays caused the critics to give scant attention to these lyric poems until well on in the nineteenth century, though Malone in the eighteenth century rightly esteemed them. And for the last hundred years successive editors have acclaimed the *Sonnets* for their poetry as well as for their kin-

ship to the plays. Some of them have appealed
to readers because of their wise comment on
life, others for the beauty of their lines, and still
others by their apparent reflection of personal
emotion. The mellow enchantment of their
style, apart from their philosophy and individual sentiment, is enough to make them immortal. Thought without some beauty of expression is a chilly thing, but the *Sonnets* have the
warmth and changeful coloring of life. They
vary in content and expression from artificial
wordplay to "thoughts beyond the reaches of
our souls." In them one may find the worldly
wit of the courtier, the practical wisdom of the
jester, the world-weary questioning of Hamlet.
The *Sonnets* lyrically express bits of philosophy and imagery such as are found scattered
through the plays. One feels that the same person wrote the *Sonnets* who was the author of
*Romeo and Juliet, Measure for Measure, Ham-
let,* and *The Tempest.* Composed by a younger
Shakespeare, the *Sonnets* have in themselves,
actually or potentially, all the elements that
reached full fruition in the plays. The *Sonnets*
are, as it were, the burgeoning of Shakespeare's
genius.

There are in the *Sonnets,* moreover, several
clear references to the actor's art, of which

there are many in the plays. These allusions are certainly personal, for no one but a man well acquainted with the theatre would have made them. In *Sonnet XXIII*, for instance, Shakespeare compares his forgetfulness of "the perfect ceremony of love's rite," in addressing his highborn friend, to the stage fright of "an unperfect actor"

> Who with his fear is put beside his part,
> Or some fierce thing replete with too much rage,
> Whose strength's abundance weakens his own heart.

In *Sonnet CX* he refers apologetically to his roving life as a player, fearing that he may thus have cheapened himself in the eyes of his aristocratic friend:

> Alas, 'tis true I have gone here and there
> And made myself a motley to the view,
> Gored mine own thoughts, sold cheap what is most dear,
> Made old offences of affections new.

And in the next sonnet he seems to refer to the low esteem in which the actor's life was held among the socially high:

O, for my sake do you with Fortune chide,
The guilty goddess of my harmful deeds,
That did not better for my life provide
Than public means which public manners breeds.
Thence comes it that my name receives a brand,
And almost thence my nature is subdued
To what it works in, like the dyer's hand.

These sonnets, while personally enlighten-
ing, are obviously not among the great poems
of the sequence. For memorable beauty of
phrase and richness of suggestion, the following sonnets, designated by their opening lines,
should be read and reread:

Shall I compare thee to a summer's day?
Thou art more lovely and more temperate. (*18*)

When in disgrace with fortune and men's eyes,
I all alone beweep my outcast state. (*29*)

When to the sessions of sweet silent thought
I summon up remembrance of things past. (*30*)

Full many a glorious morning have I seen
Flatter the mountain-tops with sovereign
eye. (*33*)

Not marble, nor the gilded monuments
Of princes, shall outlive this powerful
rhyme. (*55*)

Like as the waves make towards the pebbled
                          shore
So do our minutes hasten to their end. (*60*)

To me, fair friend, you never can be old,
For as you were when first your eye I eyed,
Such seems your beauty still. (*104*)

When in the chronicle of wasted time
I see descriptions of the fairest wights. (*106*)

Not mine own fears, nor the prophetic soul
Of the wide world dreaming on things to
                          come. (*107*)

Let me not to the marriage of true minds
Admit impediments. Love is not love
Which alters when it alteration finds. (*116*)

Poor soul, the centre of my sinful earth,
Pressed by these rebel powers that thee
                          array. (*146*)

Two sonnets, one on absence in the spring,
the other on wintry age, may be quoted in full
as perfectly illustrating the contrast and harmony between mood and external nature. The
first is a pensive English idyl, the second an
elegy: the one is suggestive of those lines in
*Romeo and Juliet*

When well-apparelled April on the heel
Of limping winter treads;

and the other recalls the autumnal speech of
Macbeth

My way of life
Is fallen into the sere, the yellow leaf.

As pure poetry, regardless of connection in the
cycle, these two sonnets are representative of
the best nondramatic verse of Shakespeare:

From you I have been absent in the spring,
When proud-pied April dressed in all his trim
Hath put a spirit of youth in everything,
That heavy Saturn laughed and leaped with him.
Yet not the lays of birds nor the sweet smell
Of different flowers in odor and in hue
Could make me any summer's story tell,
Or from their proud lap pluck them where they
grew;
Nor did I wonder at the lily's white,
Nor praise the deep vermilion of the rose:
They were but sweet, but figures of delight,
Drawn after you, you pattern of all those.
  Yet seemed it winter still, and, you away,
  As with your shadow I with these did play. (*98*)

That time of year thou mayest in me behold
When yellow leaves, or none, or few, do hang
Upon those boughs which shake against the cold,
Bare ruined choirs, where late the sweet birds
                    sang.
In me thou seest the twilight of such day
As after sunset fadeth in the west,
Which by and by black night doth take away,
Death's second self, that seals up all in rest.
In me thou seest the glowing of such fire
That on the ashes of his youth doth lie,
As the death-bed whereon it must expire,
Consumed with that which it was nourished by.
    Thus thou perceiv'st, which makes thy love
                    more strong,
    To love that well which thou must leave ere
                    long. (73)


Shakespeare wrote more sonnets than those
included in Thorpe's collection. In two of the
early plays, *Love's Labour's Lost* and *Romeo
and Juliet*, there are sonnets. These plays were
written in the sonneteering decade, and it is
during these last ten years of the century that
the lyrical quality of certain dramas is very
marked. Besides the two just mentioned, *A
Midsummer Night's Dream* and *Richard II*
have it in a high degree. *A Midsummer Night's
Dream* abounds in verse of varied measures,

while the romantic tragedy and the history play
are deeply touched with the lyric spirit. Indeed, throughout the plays of the great dramatist are injected stanzas, to be spoken or sung,
which relieve the stretches of purely dramatic
verse. Sometimes the song is the expression of a
joyous or melancholy mood, sometimes it is
a serenade or a requiem, and sometimes it is a
greeting to an entering character or a graceful
accompaniment to a change of scene. In general, the sung lyric is ornamental; it has little
or no dramatic significance. There are sixty or
more songs in Shakespeare's plays and a vast
number of spoken lyrics. The comedies have
more lyric verse than the tragedies, and the
histories very little. Most of the songs in the
plays are Shakespeare's own, but occasionally
he adopts, with modifications, a popular ballad
or some other song of the day, as, for instance,
"King Stephen was a worthy peer" and the
"willow song" in *Othello*, snatches of song by
Ophelia and the gravediggers in *Hamlet*.

The lyric, spoken and sung, was used by
most English dramatists, from the Mystery and
Morality plays on through the Elizabethan
period. The earliest regular comedies, *Ralph
Roister Doister* and *Gammer Gurton's Needle*,
have songs, the most racy of which is the drink-

ing catch in the latter play, "Back and sides, go bare, go bare." The court and university plays of John Lyly have many beautiful songs, and after him almost every popular playwright, from George Peele to Ben Jonson and Beaumont and Fletcher, made the lyric an indispensable feature of the drama. The song in the drama manifested itself musically to such an extent as to justify the assertion that the Elizabethans were "a nest of singing birds." Many of these songs were independent lyrics, but hundreds of others originally appeared in the prose romances and the drama, the two literary forms in which the imagination abundantly flowered. Sir Philip Sidney and Thomas Lodge, for instance, decorated their romances with pleasing lyrics, and the playwrights followed suit. In liberally sprinkling his plays with the seasoning of song Shakespeare was only following a prevailing practice. The Elizabethans were much given to instrumental and vocal expression, and many of the lyrics in the plays were set to music. References to music in Shakespeare's plays are numerous; there are said to be over three hundred.

The songs in Shakespeare's plays may be divided "into two types," as Professor Erskine points out, "regular stanza-forms with strong popular rhythms, and irregular cadences in which the great poet achieves his most individual effects." Examples of the more regular arrangement include "Who is Silvia?" in *Two Gentlemen of Verona*, and "O mistress mine," in *Twelfth Night;* and of the less regular, "Tell me where is fancy bred," in *The Merchant of Venice*, and "Hark! hark! the lark," the morning song in *Cymbeline*. Two dirges have the effect of a requiem, the one in *Cymbeline*, "Fear no more the heat o' the sun," and that in *The Tempest*, "Full fathom five thy father lies." In these two lyrics, as in so many of Shakespeare's, the sound and the sense perfectly harmonize, and the cadenced conclusion is like a solemn benediction. For sheer musical quality, a perfect combination of meaning and sound, attended by a haunting sense of remembered kisses, that short lyric in *Measure for Measure* has no equal in Elizabethan verse:

> Take, O, take those lips away,
>     That so sweetly were forsworn;
> And those eyes, the break of day,
>     Lights that do mislead the morn:
> But my kisses bring again,
>         Bring again;
> Seals of love, but sealed in vain,
>         Sealed in vain.

Shakespeare's songs are all short and the best of them are expressions of different moods. They express the poignancy of joy or pain as experienced in a fleeting emotion. Concreteness of imagery and beauty of phrasing distinguish them. The songs in Shakespeare's plays have a "natural magic" unequaled in the Elizabethan drama.

"King Eugenius of Scotland causes his Ancestors Histories to be Written." From Holinshed's *Chronicles*

## SHAKESPEAREAN LANGUAGE

THE language used by Shakespeare in his plays and poems, though differing somewhat in pronunciation and diction from ours, is essentially the same. In general, Elizabethan English had a greater freedom and vigor of expression than modern English. As the language gained in scientific precision, it lost the picturesqueness of sixteenth-century prose. Mod-

ern English is able to express finer shades of
thought, but it lacks the vigor of the language
of Shakespeare's day. Language varies, however, with individual taste and ability; a great
writer makes the language almost as much as
the language determines his form of expression.
In Shakespeare's plays we find poetry and prose
typical of the period and at the same time
highly individual — what we have come to call
"Shakespearean" — for the great dramatist was
a master of prose as well as of verse. We sometimes forget that Shakespeare's plays contain
some of the best Elizabethan prose. The significant changes in the meanings of certain
words in the plays since his time may be easily
learned. One may, indeed, understand and enjoy Shakespeare without knowing the contemporary meaning of all the words or the sense of
some rather vague and confused sentences, so
basically modern is Elizabethan English. Moreover, Shakespeare's vast vocabulary and his
manner of expression have had such an im-
mense influence on our speech and literature
that we are traditionally familiar with many of
his words and phrases, just as we are supposed
to recognize quotations from that other great
English classic, the King James version of the
Bible.

Many pages might be filled with expressions in our language today which are derived either from Shakespeare or through him (for some were already proverbial), but a few will illustrate how Shakespearean we are in common usage. The following might almost be described as "household words" (itself a Shakespearean phrase): "tower of strength," "yeoman service," "to the manner born," "full of sound and fury," "metal more attractive," "a Daniel come to judgment," "to wear one's heart upon one's sleeve," "to out-Herod Herod," "coign of vantage," "the sere and yellow leaf," "a touch of nature," "the quality of mercy," "hoist with his own petard," "though last, not least," "strange bedfellows." One hardly knows where to stop in this familiar-quotation game which might be extended into a book of "wit and wisdom" from the foremost English classic.

Shakespeare coined words, compounded words, and freely used one part of speech for another. Some of his compounds are striking: *pigeon-livered* (cowardly), *muddy-mettled* (irresolute), *cloud-capped, heaven-kissing, sea-swallowed.* In the last act of *The Merchant of Venice* Lorenzo and Jessica have a dialogue in which each one tries to outdo the other by recalling something romantic that happened "in such a night"; but after the fifth "in such a night" of the jesting game, Jessica says:

> I would *out-night* you, did nobody come;
> But, hark, I hear the footing of a man.

Shakespeare was fond of unusual compounds with *out-*, such as *out-tongue* ("out-tongue his complaints"), *outvenom* ("outvenoms all the worms of Nile"), *outvillain* ("outvillained villainy so far"), and *outvoice* ("outvoice the deep-mouthed sea"). Like other writers of his time he employed many words from Latin which retained their original meaning; one of the most common of these is *continent* (receptacle), as in Hamlet's remark that the small army of Fortinbras go to their death for a plot of ground "Which is not tomb enough and continent to hide the slain." Another word is *admiration* (wonder), as when Hamlet is told that his behavior has struck his mother "into amazement and admiration." In *Twelfth Night* Sir Andrew says to Viola in his challenge, "Wonder not, nor admire not in thy mind." As in the Prayer Book ("acknowledge and confess"), so also in Shakespeare, two words meaning the same thing, one from Latin and the other English, are sometimes used together. A few of the

most common words in Shakespeare which
have different meanings today are the following: *abuse* (deceive), *discover* (reveal), *doubt*
(fear, suspect), *fond* (foolish), *honest* (chaste,
honorable), *humour* (whim, caprice; originally
moisture from one of the four bodily fluids supposedly determining temperament), *influence*
(planetary power over mortals), *jealousy* (suspicion), *let* (hinder), *modest* (moderate), *owe*
(own), *practice* (plot), *prevent* (anticipate),
*remorse* (pity, compassion), *silly* (simple), *still*
(always), *success* (result, outcome), *temper-
ance* (moderation), *toys* (trifles), *unkind* (unnatural), *wit* (intellectual power, keenness of
perception).

The use of one part of speech for another
is common — adjectives for adverbs, nouns
turned into verbs. "But you, my sinews, grow
not *instant* old," exclaims Hamlet after listening to the Ghost; "some will *dear* abide it,"
says a citizen in *Julius Caesar*, referring to Caesar's death. And adverbs as nouns are frequent: "In the dark *backward* and abysm of
time" (Prospero to Miranda in *The Tempest*);
"Thou losest *here* a better *where* to find" (the
King of France to Cordelia in *King Lear*).
There are, of course, many older forms of
words, such as the *-eth* ending in the present

singular, which the modern reader promptly accepts. The use of our masculine *his* for the neuter *its*, however, is sometimes confusing, until we realize that in Old English *his* was both the masculine and neuter possessive case and generally used in the sixteenth and well on into the seventeenth century. *Its* as possessive is said to occur first in 1598 in Florio's translation of Montaigne, and there are a few instances of it in Shakespeare; but *it* (without the *s*) is found a number of times. "It lifted up it head," says Hamlet of the Ghost; and in *King Lear* the Clown remarks —

> The hedge-sparrow fed the cuckoo so long,
> That it had *it* head bit off by *it* young —

where we get a nominative and two possessives. *Its* is not found in the original King James version of the Bible, *his* being regularly used for the neuter; and *its* occurs only three times in Milton, who belonged to the generation after Shakespeare.

Though Shakespeare's vocabulary has a considerable percentage of classical words, mostly of Latin origin, it is overwhelmingly native if one counts a given word every time it occurs. All the most famous speeches in the plays have a concreteness of imagery which is best achieved by the use of native words, slightly seasoned with words of foreign derivation. The speech may be stately, or formal, or it may be highly imaginative; in either case the dramatist, by an apt use of native and derivative words, makes you see and feel what he is saying. Portia's "quality of mercy" speech in *The Merchant of Venice* (IV, 1) is stately, and yet her elaboration of that classical phrase in familiar terms of human and divine personality brings an abstraction out of the head to the heart. Brushing aside legal technicalities for the moment, Portia delivers a little sermon on the divinity of mercy, clinching her appeal to Shylock by referring him to the Lord's Prayer, a reference which her audience understood better than Shylock. Quite as effective, though in a wholly different tone, is the lyrical speech of Oberon to Puck in *A Midsummer Night's Dream* (II, 1) about "a fair vestal thronèd by the west" (Queen Elizabeth) who, disregarding Cupid's fiery shaft, passed on "in maiden meditation, fancy-free." This very imaginative speech is a happy mingling of classical and native diction, the mythological allusions in which were more intelligible to a sixteenth-century audience than to a modern. But pas-

Henry V (Laurence Olivier) woos Katharine while her
duenna watches. From Olivier's photoplay, *Henry V*

sages like this, so common in the more romantic plays, still charm by their pictorial quality. The great tragedies abound in poignant utterances touched with pathetic fatefulness, such as many of Othello's speeches and those of old King Lear to Cordelia in the shadow of death. And for picturesque concreteness, shrewdness, and vigor, consider the reply of Macbeth to his wife when she urges him to be content with his murder of Duncan, a passage that bristles with short Anglo-Saxon words which give a dreadful pungency to Macbeth's speech. Only seven or eight of these words are from the Latin:

We have scotched the snake, not killed it.
She'll close, and be herself, whilst our poor malice
Remains in danger of her former tooth.
But let the frame of things disjoint, both the
          worlds suffer,
Ere we will eat our meal in fear and sleep
In the affliction of these terrible dreams
That shake us nightly.

It is remarkable that Shakespeare's language was so little Latinized in an age marked by large importations of classical words. The Renaissance, be it remembered, was marked by an awakening of interest in the classic tongues and the Romance literatures rooted in them, and when Shakespeare began to write, the English Renaissance was at its height. That he was not more deeply touched by this foreign influx was partly because he was not a formally educated man, having had no university training like Chapman and Jonson. These two so stiffened their plays with classical phrasing that they have never been as widely heard or read as those of their great contemporary. Dryden's acute remark that Jonson "did a little too much Romanize our tongue" helps to account for the unpopularity of his plays, which, to the modern reader, seem overloaded with learning. Shakespeare's older contemporary John Lyly (it was his grandfather who wrote the Latin grammar) so infused the language of his plays and romances with classical rhetoric and allusion that he became notorious for his highly affected style. "Euphuism," the term by which we know that sort of writing today, is derived from his stilted prose romance *Euphues*. Shakespeare may be satirizing Lyly in his early play, *Love's Labour's Lost*. It is more likely, however, that he is having fun at the expense of the pedants of his day with their Latinisms and other affectations of speech. He may have wished to expose these extravagances of Elizabethan culture by injecting into a romantic

play a few of the qualities of the "comedy of
humours," a dramatic species in which Ben Jonson was a master. At any rate, several persons
in *Love's Labour's Lost* are highly "humorous"
in the Elizabethan sense. That "humour" is a
passion for using scholastic Latin.

The talk of the schoolmaster Holofernes, the
fantastical Spaniard Armado, and the curate
Nathaniel is stuffed with classical terminology.
Here is an example, taken from the opening dialogue of the fifth act of *Love's Labour's Lost*,
in which Nathaniel exchanges views with Holofernes on Armado the Spaniard:

> *Nath.* I praise God for you, sir: your rea-
> sons at dinner have been sharp and senten-
> tious; pleasant without scurrility, witty
> without affection [affectation], auda-
> cious without impudency, learned without
> opinion [dogmatism], and strange with-
> out heresy. I did converse this quondam
> day with a companion of the king's, who is
> intituled, nominated, or called, Don Adri-
> ano de Armado.
>
> *Hol.* Novi hominem tanquam te: his hu-
> mour is lofty, his discourse peremptory,
> his tongue filed, his eye ambitious, his gait
> majestical, and his general behaviour vain,
> ridiculous, and thrasonical [boastful]. He

is too picked, too spruce, too affected, too
cold, as it were, too peregrinate, as I may
call it.

*Nath.* A most singular and choice epithet.

*Hol.* He draweth out the thread of his ver-
bosity finer than the staple of his argument.

Then schoolmaster Holofernes goes on to give
a lesson in orthography. After much of this
Latinized English, the reader agrees with Moth,
Armado's page, when he says in an aside to
Costard, the Clown:

They have been at a great feast of languages,
and stolen the scraps.

To which the clown replies:

O, they have lived long on the alms-basket of
words.

Shakespeare may have lived a while on the
alms-basket of Renaissance importations, but
"the staple of his argument" comes from that
"well of English undefiled" that Chaucer and
Spenser also drew from.

The extraordinary range and variety of
Shakespeare's vocabulary may be explained in
part by his wide general reading and his association with all sorts and conditions of men. Ac-

quaintance with various types of Londoners
— noblemen, travelers, adventurers, actors,
tradesmen — was itself a liberal education for a
keenly observant dramatic genius like Shakespeare. It is a mistake to assume that an aca-
demically trained person necessarily has a more
varied vocabulary than a self-educated man.
John Milton, the Cambridge-bred poet, had
vastly more classical learning than Shakespeare
but a much smaller vocabulary. Several of
Shakespeare's contemporaries in the drama,
with no more formal education than the man of
Stratford, wrote plays of great popular appeal
and lasting merit which are distinguished by
richness and variety of language. Thomas Dekker and John Webster, for instance, were not
college-bred, and yet Dekker's comedies and
Webster's tragedies approach Shakespeare's in
verbal range and expression. *The Shoemaker's
Holiday* is one of the great English comedies,
and *The Duchess of Malfi* is among the best
Elizabethan tragedies. Dekker's and Webster's
education was very much the same as Shakespeare's. A century later one of the most pro-
lific of English prose writers, Daniel Defoe,
who never attended a university, had a vocabulary more vital and varied than his academic
contemporaries. And Defoe's older fellow Eng-

lishman, the tinker John Bunyan, who knew few books, somehow managed to acquire a very considerable stock of effective words. In American literature three outstanding writers, Melville, Whitman, and Mark Twain, have shown how genius may, without benefit of academic guidance, demonstrate the flexibility, raciness, and reach of their native tongue. That is what Shakespeare has done in language which is a composite of classical Saxon elements.

As drama is primarily spoken, it may be interesting to have some idea of how the language of the plays sounded on the stage. How was Elizabethan English pronounced? Would an English-speaking person of today have understood an actor of Shakespeare's time? Probably so, but not without difficulty. The intonation was, of course, somewhat different, and the pronunciation of certain words has changed. Englishmen and Americans of today speak the same language, but with a different accent, or intonation, and occasionally with a different pronunciation, though they have little trouble in understanding each other. Modern British English is orally nearer Elizabethan speech than American English, but various changes over three hundred years have wrought phonetic differences. The consonants were sounded in

Shakespeare's day much as they are in ours, with several exceptions: *g* and *k* were heard in words like *gnash, knee,* and *knife; l* was sounded in *should, would,* and *folk,* and the letter *r* was more trilled than is usual in modern English. The vowels varied considerably: *a* had a broader sound than today; *o* in words like *cold* and *bold* and *old* had the sound of *au* (*aw*), as often in modern British English; *ea* sounded like *a* in *fame* (still heard in the eighteenth century when *tea* was pronounced *tay*); *ay* and *ai* sounded much like long *i,* according to which the words *day* and *say* would be pronounced *die* and *sigh; ou* was sometimes *oo,* as in *house* (*hoos*), and sometimes *au* (*aw*), as in *soul* (*sawl*) and *now* (*naw*). The endings -*tion* and -*sion* were often pronounced as two syllables especially in verse ("Seeking the bubble reputation"; "And I did laugh sans intermission"), where the meter requires the prolongation. Words like *vengeance, ocean, courtier,* were sometimes lengthened into three syllables, and monosyllables like *dear, more,* and *lord,* into two. The familiar word *alarm* becomes *alarum* by trilling the *r.* Many words in Shakespeare have either a variable, or regularly different, accent from that of today: *revénue, óbscure, cómplete, perséver, sécure, aspéct, énvy, distinct, sinister.* A feeling for rhythm will generally enable the reader to give the proper metrical accent to syllables, as it will guide him in pronouncing the final *-ed* in verbs. Modern editions of Shakespeare usually indicate by an apostrophe ('d) when the *-ed* is not separately pronounced. In these two lines from *Love's Labour's Lost* it is a distinct syllable:

> But love, first learnèd in a lady's eyes,
> Lives not alone immurèd in the brain.

In the following colorful passage from *Antony and Cleopatra* (Cleopatra's dream of her dead hero) are illustrations of sounded and silent final *-ed:*

> His legs bestrid the ocean: his rear'd arm
> Crested the world: his voice was propertied
> As all the tunèd spheres, and that to friends;
> But when he meant to quail and shake the orb,
> He was as rattling thunder. For his bounty,
> There was no winter in't; an autumn 'twas
> That grew the more by reaping: his delights
> Were dolphin-like; they show'd his back above
> The elements they liv'd in: in his livery
> Walk'd crowns and crownets, realms and islands were
> As plates dropp'd from his pocket.

The cottage in which Anne Hathaway, Shakespeare's
wife, is supposed to have grown up

## SHAKESPEAREAN VERSE

SHAKESPEARE and the other Elizabethan dramatists wrote their plays for the
most part in blank verse, that is, in unrhymed
five-foot lines of normally ten syllables, with
the accent, or stress, on the even syllables. The
"foot" consisted of an unstressed and a stressed
syllable, technically known as "iambic" and the
line as "iambic pentameter" (a name derived
from classical meter). Here is a perfectly regular line from *Hamlet:*

But look, the morn in russet mantle clad.

Read naturally, the accent falls, as indicated, on the even syllables. The same is true in the following quotation from *Henry IV, Part One* (Hotspur's speech):

> O géntlemén, the tíme of lífe is shórt.
> To spénd that shórtness básely wére too lóng
> If lífe did ríde upón a díal's póint.

This measure was inherited by Shakespeare from certain predecessors. The earliest of those to use it in the drama were two mediocre poets, Sackville and Norton, in their tragedy of *Gorboduc*, or *Ferrex and Porrex* (1562). Shakespeare's early contemporary, Christopher Marlowe, was the first to employ blank verse with high distinction, but Shakespeare gave it variety and flexibility. As blank verse became a favorite with many English poets, it is regarded as the standard measure, more popular in dramatic and epic poetry than in any other. Next in general use was the older rhyming couplet, with the same number of accents and syllables, as in these two lines from *Hamlet:*

> I múst be crúel, ónly tó be kínd;
> Thus bád begíns, and wórse remáins behínd.

But perfect metrical regularity would soon become monotonous, and no great poet has ever been "regular." One must not think of Shakespeare as consciously measuring his verse by any rule of thumb, concerning himself as to how the accents fell. What he did concern himself with was the rhythm in general, perhaps subconsciously achieving variety without violating a larger uniformity of pattern. It is likely that in his earlier experience in writing blank verse he thought more about technical regularity, just as a young musician is apt to take less liberty with his score than an older one. At any rate, Shakespeare's earlier blank verse shows much greater regularity than his later, though even in a very early play like *The Comedy of Errors* he is never mechanically "correct." Compare, for example, the following passages: the first is from *The Comedy of Errors* (Adriana's speech to Antipholus) and the second from the late play, *Cymbeline* (Imogen's soliloquy).

The time was once when thou unurg'd wouldst
               vow
That never words were music to thine ear,
That never object pleasing to thine eye,
That never touch well welcome to thy hand,
That never meat sweet-savour'd in thy taste,

Unless I spake, or look'd, or touch'd, or carv'd to
      thee.
How comes it now, my husband, O, how comes it,
That thou art then estranged from thyself?
Thyself I call it, being strange to me,
That, undividable, incorporate,
Am better than thy dear self's better part.

Read this speech aloud and you will feel that
the scansion is regular, though not monotonous.
One line, the sixth, has an extra foot, the seventh has an extra syllable. Now read the following aloud and note the difference:

I see a man's life is a tedious one:
I have tir'd myself, and for two nights together
Have made the ground my bed. I should be sick,
But that my resolution helps me. Milford,
When from the mountain-top Pisanio show'd
      thee,
Thou wast within a ken. O Jove! I think
Foundations fly the wretched; such, I mean,
Where they should be relieved. Two beggars
      told me
I could not miss my way: will poor folks lie,
That have afflictions on them, knowing 'tis
A punishment or trial? Yes; no wonder.

The blank verse of this last selection reads more
like prose, though the general rhythm is pre-

served and several lines are quite regular. Five
lines have eleven syllables each and four run
over into the next.

But the most noteworthy variations from the
normal in the dramatic verse are in the change
from the iambic to some other measure and in
the number of pauses to the line. The foot most
commonly substituted for the iambic is the
trochaic, consisting of an accented and an unaccented syllable. While this substitution may
occur anywhere in the line, it is more frequently found in the beginning. The following
short passage from *Julius Caesar* has several
trochaic feet:

Háted by óne he lóves, bráv'd by his bróther,
Check'd like a bondman; all his faults observ'd,
Set in a note-book, learn'd and conn'd by rote,
To cast into my teeth. O, I could weep
My spirit from mine eyes! — There is my dagger,
And here my naked breast; within, a heart
Dearer than Plutus' mine, richer than gold.

It will be noted, when read aloud, that this
speech owes its easy naturalness in no small degree to the mingling of the iambic and the
trochaic feet, the pauses, the two double ("feminine") endings, and the two run-on lines.

Hamlet instructs the players who have come to Elsinore Castle. From Olivier's photoplay, *Hamlet*

Sometimes we find an extra, unstressed syllable, making the iambic foot an anapaest (two unaccented and one accented syllable), as in this line from *Hamlet:*

I am móre an ántique Róman thán a Dáne.

In speaking this line, however, the actor may have unconsciously made the first foot iambic by contraction, *I'm more*. But in the following line the third foot seems unmistakably anapaestic:

Of ímpious stúbbornness; 'tís unmánly gríef.

Two stressed syllables in immediate succession (spondee) frequently occur, thus:

Cóme, cóme, and sít you dówn; you sháll not búdge.

In the following lines from *The Merchant of Venice* the spondees are evident:

The móon shínes bríght; in súch a níght as thís.
Díd feígn that Órpheus dréw trées, stónes, and flóods.

And old King Lear, defying the storm, cries
out in a line loaded with explosive monosyllables:

Blow, winds, and crack your cheeks! rage! blow!

The two lacking syllables are supplied by expressive pauses.

Omitted syllables under emotional stress or
in rapid, interrupted speech are fairly common
in Shakespeare, but extra-metrical syllables are
much more common and, as already intimated,
increase in frequency in the middle and later
plays. In *Hamlet*, for instance, they are numerous at the end of lines:

Whether 'tis nobler in the mind to suffer
The slings and arrows of outrageous fortune,
Or to take arms against a sea of troubles.

The normal ten-syllable line is sometimes shortened to eight or six or fewer. These short lines,
occurring at irregular intervals, render the
Ghost's long speech to Hamlet impressive by
pauses heightening Hamlet's suspense and the
agitation of both. Occasionally we come upon
twelve-syllable iambic lines in Shakespeare,
technically known as alexandrines, as these
from *The Merchant of Venice:*

To find the other forth and by advent(u)ring
both.

And the inscriptions on the caskets are six-foot
iambic, possibly to differentiate them from the
dramatic dialogue:

Who chooseth me shall get as much as he deserves.

An important matter to observe in reading
the plays is the arrangement of metrically
broken lines at the end and beginning of
speeches. A speech ending with a shortened
line is often immediately followed, especially
in rapid dialogue, by one carrying on the
thought in a brief supplementary line. This
fractional new line completes metrically the
preceding, is generally printed to the right,
after a space, and should be scanned as a part of
the last line. The following fragment of a dialogue between Brutus and Cassius will illustrate:

*Brutus.*    When Marcus Brutus grows so covet-
                              ous
                To lock such rascal counters [coins]
                       from his friends,
                Be ready, gods, with all your thunder-
                         bolts,

Dash him to pieces!

*Cassius.*                         I denied you not.

*Brutus.*    You did.

*Cassius.*            I did not; he was but a fool
That brought my answer back — Bru-
tus hath rived my heart.
A friend should bear a friend's infirmi-
ties,
But Brutus makes mine greater than
they are.

*Brutus.*    I do not, till you practise them on me.

*Cassius.*    You love me not.

*Brutus.*                        I do not like your faults.

In the several passages already used for illustration the strong, or primary, accent has been
noted. It should be borne in mind, however,
that the weak, or secondary, stress also counts
when a word of three or more syllables is involved. Many lines are shorter to the eye than
to the ear when mainly composed of classical
words. These longer words often give to the
spoken verse a pleasing resonance or solemn
stateliness. Here are several from *Hamlet:*

Absent thee from felicity awhile.

To his unmaster'd importunity.

With turbulent and dang'rous lunacy.

This bodiless creation ecstasy.

Shakespeare showed great skill in the distri-
bution of pauses in his blank verse. In the middle and later plays the pauses occur more frequently within the line than in the earlier. This
variation in the movement makes the verse more
flexible. The following typical examples, drawn
from early and later plays, will serve to show
the varying position and the length of the
pause:

Home-keeping youth have ever homely wits.
Were't not affection chains thy tender days
To the sweet glances of thy honor'd love,
I rather would entreat thy company
To see the wonders of the world abroad
Than, living dully sluggardiz'd at home,
Wear out thy youth with shapeless idleness.

(*Two Gentlemen of Verona*)

Why, all the souls that were, were forfeit once,
And He that might the vantage best have took
Found out the remedy. How would you be
If He, which is the top of judgment, should
But judge you as you are? O, think on that!
And mercy then will breathe within your lips.

(*Measure for Measure*)

Nay, pray you seek no color for your going,
But bid farewell and go. When you su'd staying,
Then was the time for words. No going then!
Eternity was in our lips and eyes,
Bliss in our brows' bent, none our parts so poor
But was a race of heaven. They are so still,
Or thou, the greatest soldier of the world,
Art turned the greatest liar.

(Antony and Cleopatra)

It should be added, however, that in general
the duration and frequency of the pause will
depend upon the nature of the speech, whether
emotional, argumentative, or simply conversational.

The songs and other lyrics in Shakespeare
are mostly in trochaic measure, with many iambic lines. The lines vary in length from two to
five stresses, but the prevailing number is four.
The following stanza from the "Dirge in Cymbeline," though structurally more regular than
some others, is fairly representative, metrically,
of lyric verse in the plays. It will be noted that
the last line is iambic:

Fear no more the heat o' the sun
And the furious winter's rages;
Thou thy worldly task hast done,

Home art gone and ta'en thy wages:
Golden lads and girls all must,
As chimney-sweepers, come to dust.

The *Sonnets* show the same stresses as blank verse but have alternate rhymes and a concluding couplet.

While one may enjoy Shakespeare without a knowledge of meter, some acquaintance with the elements of versification is desirable for a full understanding of his poetry. If one has a sense for rhythm, the metrical appreciation of poetry is easy. To scan Shakespearean verse one should read the lines slowly, letting the accents, or stresses, fall naturally. As already indicated, each line should have five of these, but may occasionally have four or six. Usually the metrical stress in a word coincides with the spoken and is the same in verse as it is in prose. What makes verse is the rhythmical, alternating sequence of vocal stress. One should avoid forcing the pronunciation to fit a preconceived pattern. Allowing for certain differences in Elizabethan and modern pronunciation, one should read the line as one might read it in prose; it is the poet's business to have made it poetry. The natural intonation in reading will ordinarily result in the proper metrical interpretation of Shakespeare's verse. Monotony is avoided by accepting minor irregularities as "regular." In silent reading one should mentally hear the beats, feel the lilt in the lines. This is, of course, easier in rhetorical passages, where the movement resembles the impassioned eloquence of oratorical prose, and in romantic utterances of heightened imagery. The suitors' speeches in *The Merchant of Venice*, and those of Henry V to his army, are examples of the first; the balcony scene in *Romeo and Juliet* and the pastoral scenes in *As You Like It* and *The Winter's Tale* are lyrical in expression. All these are essentially poetic in matter and manner.

Undue emphasis may, of course, be put upon versification in Shakespeare; too much attention may be paid to the mere mechanics of verse. It is well, however, to understand how and why "verse tests" form an important internal evidence of the approximate date of a play. These tests, as already explained, have been carefully worked out. But too great concern with the technicalities of meter would mean shifting the interest from the play itself. After all, the play's the thing. The plot and characters are the matters about which the audience in the theatre is wholly concerned. Very

few of the men and women listening to a play
think of it as poetry. Now and then an accomplished actor or actress, sensitive to the rhythm
of the lines spoken, touches them with enchantment for the ear: Edwin Booth did it and Ellen
Terry did it. For the reader, who *sees* the verse,
there is an added satisfaction in scanning the
lines audibly or inaudibly: he may imagine the
action through both his mind's eye and his
mind's ear. Those who read Shakespeare for
his "philosophy" simply want the meaning of
the speeches, which they too often regard as
the dramatist's personal sentiments. They care
little about the form, except that wisdom is
more easily remembered when put up in neat,
portable packages. But for those who read
Shakespeare, as he should be read, primarily for
his dramatic and poetic interpretation of human life, some knowledge of verse technique
will aid in the appreciation of the plays as literature. And it is this aesthetic enjoyment of
Shakespeare that has kept his plays on the stage
and on the library shelves.

Three of Shakespeare's signatures, from the three briefs
of the will in the Prerogative Court

# THE ESSENTIAL SHAKESPEARE

THE plays of Shakespeare manifestly differ
in dramatic and aesthetic interest. Of the
thirty-seven or thirty-eight usually included in
"complete" editions of his works perhaps not
more than half have been generally read and reread, and fewer still have been favorites on the
stage. One-volume editions of Shakespeare for
schools usually include from twenty to twenty-
three, arranged in the order of the dramatist's
development. Such collections are likely to be-
gin with *The Comedy of Errors* or *A Midsummer Night's Dream* and end with *The
Tempest*. They generally omit *Love's Labour's
Lost*, *Two Gentlemen of Verona*, *Titus An-*

*dronicus, Henry VI* (three parts), *King John, Taming of the Shrew, Merry Wives of Windsor, All's Well,* and *Troilus and Cressida,* from the early and middle periods; *Timon of Athens,* and the partly Shakespearean plays *Pericles, Henry VIII,* and *Two Noble Kinsmen,* from the later period. Some of these have not been included among Shakespeare's "principal" or more widely read plays because they are either immature or only in part by the great dramatist; others have been left out because they are "disagreeable," like the bloody and brutal *Titus Andronicus* or the coarse and cynical *All's Well* and *Troilus and Cressida.* The three parts of *Henry VI* seem to have been written in collaboration by several persons, one of whom was Shakespeare. The external evidence of Shakespeare's part authorship is the inclusion of *Henry VI* in the First Folio (1623). The internal evidence of Shakespeare's collaboration is found in the style and meter of certain scenes. One of these is the quarrel scene in the Temple Garden (Part I, act ii, 4) and the plucking of the red and white roses. This is quite in the Shakespearean manner. Several of the plays frequently omitted from the one-volume collections for students or general readers may have been so thoroughly revised by Shakespeare as

to be mainly his work. Collaboration and revision may have been carried on at the same
time. The omission, therefore, of a given play
from a representative collection may be due
quite as much to the nature of the plot as to
the conviction that the play is the product of
several hands.

It is not to be inferred, however, that the less
known and less read plays are distinctly in-
ferior in plot and characterization. Some of
them abound in thrilling action and lifelike
characters. *The Taming of the Shrew* and *The
Merry Wives of Windsor*, for instance, are
lively farces rather than pure comedies; they
hold the attention chiefly by the action. *King
John* has some great speeches and tense mo-
ments. *Two Gentlemen of Verona*, though
psychologically weak, has much pleasing dialogue and one of the loveliest lyrics in Shakespeare, "Who is Silvia?" In this play, moreover, we meet Shakespeare's first professional
clown, Launce. *Love's Labour's Lost* is mostly
situation rather than action; the dialogue, sometimes brilliant, seems imitative of that in John
Lyly's court comedies. *Timon of Athens*, the
tragedy of a man turned into a man hater by
the ingratitude of professed friends, is a very
uneven play which is strongly Shakespearean

only in the last two acts. Less than half of *Henry VIII*, though the play is in the First Folio, is thought to be by Shakespeare. Much of the verse is like John Fletcher's, and the two most famous speeches in the play — Wolsey's farewell to greatness and his advice to Thomas Cromwell ("Cromwell, I charge thee, fling away ambition") — are now attributed to Fletcher. *The Two Noble Kinsmen*, not in the Folios but first published in 1634 as "by John Fletcher and William Shakespeare," is of course a joint product. Judging by style and versification, critics have been able to identify those parts of *The Two Noble Kinsmen* written by Shakespeare. Such lines as the following, for instance, are distinctly Shakespearean. They are taken from the scene (I, i) in which the three queens, whose unburied husbands were slain by King Creon of Thebes, plead with Duke Theseus of Athens to allow them burial:

> O, pity, duke!
> Thou purger of the earth, draw thy fear'd sword
> That does good turns to the world; give us the bones
> Of our dead kings, that we may chapel them;
> And of thy boundless goodness, take some note
> That for our crowned heads we have no roof

Save this, which is the lion's and the bear's,
And vault to everything.

*Pericles*, included in the Third Folio (1664), is certainly in part by Shakespeare (perhaps most of Acts III, IV, and V), but who collaborated with him is not positively known.

Besides these plays, in which it seems certain that Shakespeare had a considerable share, there are six others which were at one time attributed to him and published, along with *Pericles*, in the second printing of the Third Folio. Still other anonymous plays of the time have been credited to Shakespeare, but without any convincing evidence. All these so-called Shakespearean dramas constitute the "Shakespeare Apocrypha" about which scholars have done much futile guessing. In a day of extensive collaboration among playwrights and of little pride in authorship, the authorship of many plays remained doubtful. Only those which have external-internal evidence of Shakespeare's participation have been included in the authorized editions of the great dramatist. Fantastic attempts to prove that somebody else wrote all the Shakespeare plays may continue, but such efforts, however ingenious and plausible to the unskilled, will doubtless continue to impress competent judges as pathetic examples of misdirected energy.

Dryden's remark, about fifty years after the great dramatist's death, that Shakespeare "was the man who of all modern, and perhaps ancient, poets, had the largest and most comprehensive soul" has already been quoted. In the eighteenth century Dr. Samuel Johnson declared that the seventeenth-century French dramatist Corneille was to Shakespeare as "a clipped hedge is to a forest." In the early nineteenth century the German Goethe spoke of Shakespeare as "a great psychologist," and Coleridge referred to him as "myriad-minded." Many books have been written on him as a thinker and dramatic artist; political and ethical philosophers have drawn heavily on his works for illustrations. The history plays have been closely studied by political theorizers and the great tragedies by moralists. Shakespeare's skill as a dramatic technician has been emphasized by modern critics, who have rightly felt that a practical playwright could be completely understood only through a knowledge of the conditions under which he worked. These have thought of the poet-dramatist as also a craftsman whose mind and art should be judged in connection with the requirements of

the contemporary theatre and professional acting. All these varied kinds of emphasis show the
great range of Shakespeare's thinking and the
almost infinite variety of his accomplishment.
But where and how, it may be asked, is the
"essential Shakespeare" most clearly revealed?
Is it in the histories, the comedies, or the tragedies? In other words, which of the three groups
is most "original"?

In the seven plays drawn from English history there is manifestly less originality in plot
and characterization than in the comedies and
tragedies proper. The dramatist is limited in the
history plays; he must in general follow the
chronicles. He has less freedom in plot construction and even in delineation of character
than in dramas whose sources are traditionally
romantic. There is, moreover, in the stories of
kingship a sameness of action and fate which,
though it gives a certain unity to the historical
plays, makes them as a group essentially epic in
character. The episodic movement in the narrative is not perfectly adapted to the demands of
dramatic technique. But despite the danger of
making a type character of a royal person,
Shakespeare generally succeeds in humanizing
him. This understanding of the king as a man,
along with the sufferings entailed by his hu-

manity, is often shown in royal speeches in which the king allies himself with common men. Richard II, who strongly believed in the sanctity of kingship, sums up the fate of monarchs in most historical plays:

For God's sake, let us sit upon the ground
And tell sad stories of the death of kings:
How some have been deposed; some slain in war;
Some haunted by the ghosts they have deposed;
Some poisoned.

And then he says to his accusers, whom he charges with mock reverence in his presence:

Throw away respect,
Tradition, form, and ceremonious duty;
For you have but mistook me all this while:
I live with bread like you, feel want, taste grief,
Need friends: subjected thus,
How can you say to me I am a king?

Perhaps the best illustration of democratic feeling and association in royalty is found in Henry V's conversations with his soldiers on the night before the Battle of Agincourt. Unrecognized by his men, King Henry answers the questions of one of them about kings:

For though I speak it to you, I think the
King is but a man, as I am: the violet smells
to him as it does to me, the element [sky]
shows to him as it doth to me; all his senses
have but human conditions: his ceremonies
laid by, in his nakedness he appears but a
man.

And Henry V, be it remembered, is Shakespeare's ideal king, the only one of his monarchs who may rightly be called heroic.

Some of the histories have comic subplots or
scenes which serve to relieve the monotony of
the speeches in the higher social group. The
play in which this humorous diversion is most
used is *Henry IV*, with Falstaff and his tavern
associates who are linked to the serious plot by
Prince Hal. This comedy strand in the play is
Shakespeare's own invention, Falstaff his immortal creation. So popular was Sir John with
his creator and the public that the dramatist
carried him through the two parts and reluc-
tantly parted with him in a pathetic account of
his death in *Henry V*, only to revive him (it is
said by royal command) in a rollicking farce,
*The Merry Wives of Windsor*. Indeed, it is
Falstaff who has kept *Henry IV* on the stage;
he, and not the king, is the hero of the play; he
and Prince Hal and their companions vitalize

the action and dialogue. Without this Hamlet-in-reverse, *Henry IV* would be a chronicle play of factional strife. Other historical plays have little or no comic relief: *Richard III*, an early play in the Marlowe tradition, has sardonic humor, but little else to relieve the villainy of bloody tragedy; *King John* has the pathos of youthful innocence sacrificed to royal ambition; *Richard II* is a tragic exhibition of royal weakness relieved only by the lyric beauty of a poet-king's speeches; and *Henry V*, most heroic of the history plays, has touches of comedy in the soldier group, the Falstaff survivals, and the wooing of Princess Katherine in broken French and English. All these "humanizing" elements in the histories may be regarded as original contributions of the great dramatist. The most essentially Shakespearean of the history group are *Richard II*, *Henry IV*, and *Henry V*.

In his earliest comedies — *The Comedy of Errors, Love's Labour's Lost, Two Gentlemen of Verona* — Shakespeare seems to have been experimenting. The plots are conventional and the characterization is more or less imitative, following the inherited Renaissance pattern. The mechanical regularity of the action, the balancing of scenes one against another, and the confusions of identity were fine exercises in the art of plot construction for a beginner. Shipwrecks, separations of families, and final reunions were thrilling episodes in these Renaissance romances which Shakespeare was to use in later plays also. Some of the persons in these classical-romantic stories are prototypes of well-developed characters in later comedies. Julia in *Two Gentlemen of Verona*, for instance, is an early heroine who will appear later as a Rosalind or a Viola. *Love's Labour's Lost* anticipates other satirical social plays of situation, while Biron and his witty companions faintly foreshadow such accomplished gentlemen as Mercutio and Benedick in subsequent plays. In these first comedies, as in all the rest, both the scenes and the people are invested with an atmosphere of Shakespeare's own familiar England.

But not until the appearance of *A Midsummer Night's Dream* and the high comedies that follow do we find the full blossoming of Shakespeare's art. *A Midsummer Night's Dream* is a complex of classical, romantic, and realistic strands skilfully woven into a larger unity. The Greek setting is really dear old England, somewhere near London, the fairies spring from British folklore, and Bottom's "rude mechanicals" are easily recognizable as homely native rustics. To fuse these incongruous elements into one harmonious whole was an astonishing feat of dramatic craftsmanship. In this play Shakespeare achieved mastery of plot construction, and he expressed himself in verse of great variety and extraordinary beauty. To have seen this romantic comedy on a moonlight night in an outdoor English setting, as it used to be played each summer in Regent's Park in London, is to have recaptured for the moment something of the buoyant joyousness of Elizabethan England. There was magic in the sight and sound of it. And one can well understand why Mendelssohn set the poetry of *A Midsummer Night's Dream* to music.

The earlier comedies are more noteworthy for situation and incident than for character. One more easily remembers the scene of action and what happens than the persons involved. The creation of memorable, clear-cut personalities in the comedies is first seen in *The Merchant of Venice, Much Ado about Nothing, As You Like It,* and *Twelfth Night. The Merchant* is almost a tragi-comedy, but the three others are "joyous comedies." Shylock has become a symbol of racial pride, avarice, and suffering ("sufferance is the badge of all our tribe"). Shakespeare's is the only Jew-baiting play that humanizes its protagonist, evoking both hatred and pity. Though Shylock undoubtedly excited the animosity of an Elizabethan audience, there must have been some present who realized that, though his inhumanity was deservedly punished, he was not all bad. That he was required to become a Christian was perhaps the worst of his penalties, but the terrible irony of it would not have been so evident to an Elizabethan as to the more tolerant modern. The other great creation in the play is Portia, the versatile, highborn lady of the Renaissance, who in mind and manner is as impressive as a heroine of courtly love, but far more human.

In the first of the joyous comedies, *Much Ado*, Benedick and Beatrice are Shakespearean originals, as are the Dogberry-Verges group. They all talk prose and are quite realistic — the sparring couple in their satirical badinage and the muddle-headed constables in their out-and-out misuse of the Queen's English. One readily remembers Benedick and Beatrice (the first has contributed a word to our speech), though one may forget the story of Hero and Claudio except that their church wedding was rudely interrupted. The greenwood setting of *As You*

*Like It* only enhances the charm of Rosalind, sophisticated pastoral lady. She and the courtly clown Touchstone and the philosophizing Jaques form an immortal trio of high comedy personages. The outdoor grace of Rosalind is matched by the indoor enchantment of Viola in *Twelfth Night*, last of the shipwrecked maidens until the later dramatized romances. Viola, the incarnation of arch, seriocomic femininity, is a study in dual or triple personality (confusion beloved of the old romancers) — page, lover, twin sister. Lower in the social scale, but strongly akin to her in wit, is Maria, with Sir Toby, who is mildly Falstaffian, and Sir Andrew, the most complete fool in Shakespeare. In these comedies Shakespeare's genius had its finest flowering in social character portrayal.

The plays which seem to foreshadow the great tragedies are the "dark comedies." These comedies do not deal primarily with revenge, ambition, jealousy, and ingratitude, as do the tragedies proper, but with such matters as faithful and fickle love, feminine persistence, and individual mercy tempering justice. Isabella in *Measure for Measure* pleading for her brother's life with Angelo is one of Shakespeare's strongest women. The theme of this "problem play," a sister's chastity weighed against an erring brother's life, affords a finer occasion for psychic revelation than is found in either *All's Well* or *Troilus and Cressida*. In the handling of the rather repellent plot of *Measure for Measure*, centering about a lustful judge, a saintly lady, and a weak brother, Shakespeare wrote a play that is essentially modern in its psychological appeal, a play which in parts is only a little below the great tragedies themselves. The scene in the third act in which the condemned brother argues for life at the sacrifice of his sister's virtue is Shakespeare at his tragic best:

*Claudio.*      Death is a fearful thing.
*Isabella.*    And shamed life a hateful.
*Claudio.*      Ay, but to die, and go we know not
                     where;
                To lie in cold obstruction and to rot;
                This sensible warm motion to become
                A kneaded clod, and the delighted spirit
                To bathe in fiery floods, or to reside
                In thrilling region of thick-ribbed ice;
                To be imprison'd in the viewless winds,
                And blown with restless violence round
                     about
                The pendent world; or to be — worse
                     than worst —

Of those that lawless and incertain thought
Imagines howling, — 'tis too horrible!
The weariest and most loathed worldly life
That age, ache, penury, and imprison-
ment
Can lay on nature is a paradise
To what we fear of death.

*Isabella.*   Alas, alas!

*Claudio.*           Sweet sister, let me live.
What sin you do to save a brother's life,
Nature dispenses with the deed so far
That it becomes a virtue.

*Isabella.*                   O you beast!
O faithless coward! O dishonest
wretch!
Wilt thou be made a man out of my
vice?
Is't not a kind of incest, to take life
From thine own sister's shame?

Characters in the last romantic comedies are
more real than much of the action in which
they are involved. The insanely jealous king in
*The Winter's Tale* is only a pale Othello, but
his wife Hermione is a vivid and spirited Desdemona, while their lost daughter, the shep-
herdess Perdita, is one of Shakespeare's most
charming girls, whose royal blood shows in her

Florizel: Thou dearest Perdita . . . I prythee darken not
the mirth o' the feast. From *The Winter's Tale*

speech and manners. And the sheep-shearing festival in which she figures as "the queen of curds and cream" is pure English, perhaps a lyric revival of what the man from Stratford had seen years ago in Warwickshire. Was the dramatist speaking his own sentiment in *The Tempest* when he makes Prospero say "The rarer action is in virtue than in vengeance"? If so, he who had earlier written much of revenge and ingratitude had attained a higher wisdom in these last plays. Is that wizard who is the deity of an enchanted island Shakespeare himself? And is the island England? Vain questions. But one inevitably fancies that in these last moonlit comedies, so serenely remote from life's actualities, Shakespeare is spiritually as well as dramatically present.

If we raise these tantalizing questions about the Shakespeare of the comedies and histories, we ask similar questions, with even greater earnestness, about the creator of *Hamlet* and *Othello* and *Macbeth* and *King Lear*. For it is in these supreme tragedies that Shakespeare went deepest into the motives back of human action. Love between man and woman, the dominant theme of comedy and one early tragedy, gives place to more worldly motives in these four mighty dramas. With the title characters it is some personal weakness or excess that destroys each one and wrecks his little world — an internal force, not the external Fate of Greek tragedy. Hamlet's extremely reflective nature, impelling him to think "too precisely on the event," delays the consummation of filial revenge. Othello's credulity, inflamed by villainous innuendo, first perplexes in the extreme a man not easily jealous and then destroys him. Macbeth's overleaping ambition involves him in a series of murders and ultimately damns him and his queen. And Lear's rash judgment in the unstable division of his kingdom leads him into a prolonged succession of domestic and political ills which recoil on the inventors' heads. Though Shakespeare found these old stories in one book or another, and two of them already crudely dramatized, he so combined the scattered material, developing and adding characters, that he made in each perfected play an original contribution. Legendary lore and history are fused, touched with comic relief, and clothed in glorious verse. In these four tragedies he attained the highest reach in the history of dramatic art.

Of the four dramas *King Lear* is the one in which Shakespeare came nearest to the spirit of Greek tragedy. The protagonist in the English play, an old man battling with the tempest in his own mind and the elemental storm without, is Sophoclean in its irony and fatefulness. The atmosphere of the play is very pagan, and the characters are Celtic in their impulsive fits and starts, more British than Saxon. What makes *King Lear* so personal to each of us is the feeling, in reading or seeing it, that in one way or another, we ourselves may know ingratitude. We may not be moved by revenge or jealousy or political ambition, but who that lives long may escape ingratitude? And the smart that comes "from benefits forgot" is so often mentioned by Shakespeare that one suspects he spoke feelingly. Of all the tragedies of Shakespeare *King Lear* is the most difficult to represent adequately on the stage, for it is too inward and too elemental to be interpreted within the time and space limitations of the playhouse. It is a drama of cosmic proportions.

In his four supreme tragedies Shakespeare transcends race and nationality and becomes universal. His most popular play affords an apt illustration of this. Hamlet is far more than a Danish or English prince. He is the philosophic intellectual not only of the Renaissance but of any time and country which has inherited the best of ancient and mediaeval culture. Poor

Ophelia, taking his strange utterances as evidence of madness, lamented the overthrow of a noble mind —

The courtier's, scholar's, soldier's, eye, tongue, sword;
The expectancy and rose of the fair state,
The glass of fashion and the mould of form,
The observed of all observers.

That is a good description of an ideal Renaissance prince; but Hamlet is to us much more than that. He is almost the symbol of the human mind functioning as poet, thinker, and moralist. There is something of Hamlet in every meditative person. In Shakespeare's works the Hamlet quality is not confined to the play of that name: it is strongly evident in the lyrical lamentations of Richard II, in the soliloquizings of Brutus, in the weary farewells of Macbeth, in Isabella's and Claudio's conversation in prison, in Prospero's last speeches, in Othello's tortured thinking, and in various sonnets. It is hardly safe to identify a great dramatist with any one of his characters, but the frequency of Hamlet-like sentiments in the plays might justify the inference that Hamlet, of all the Shakespearean characters, is most like his dramatic creator.

This inquiry into some essential Shakespearean characteristics leads to two general conclusions. The first is that while Shakespeare created few plots, he modified in various ways those that came to his hand, so transforming the original stories as to make them virtually new. This he accomplished by elimination, transposition, and addition, showing in the process expert craftsmanship and fine artistry. The second conclusion is that Shakespeare is supreme in the variety and lifelikeness of his characters. It is because of them and the transcendent merit of his poetry that his name is imperishable. His men and women give us the perfect illusion of reality. So true is this that we think and speak of them as historical persons, though most of them had only a legendary existence. And those who once actually lived, such as Shakespeare's Roman personages and English kings, are, thanks to the dramatist's art, still vividly alive. This dramatic portraiture of historical and legendary individuals often seems more authentic than the historian's, for in literature psychological truth is more effective than scientific fact. A gallery of Shakespearean characters, sculptured from the "originals" in the plays, would be to the cultured visitor an exhibition of familiar figures. Those bas-relief scenes from the plays which adorn the marble walls of the Folger Library in Washington represent beings forever alive to the imagination. Such was the extraordinary power of the poet-dramatist in creating vital characters and bestowing upon them the gift of immortality.

# *Appendix*

# A FEW METRICAL
## AND OTHER NOTES

AN EXAMINATION of Shakespeare's plays by several well-known German, English, and American scholars has resulted in certain conclusions as to the number of lines of blank and rhyming verse, amount of prose, number of run-on and end-stopped lines, light and weak endings. From these statistics only a few plays are singled out here as representing the minimum and maximum figures.

The shortest play is *The Comedy of Errors* with 1,778 lines, 1,150 of which are blank verse and 380 rhyme, and 240 lines of prose. About 13 per cent of the verse lines are run-on, and there are no light and weak endings. The next shortest play is *Macbeth* with 2,108 lines, 1,588 of which are blank verse and 118 rhyme, and 158 lines of prose. About 36 per cent of the verse is run-on, and there are 23 light and weak endings. The longest play is *Hamlet* with 3,931 lines, 2,490 of which are blank verse and 81 rhyme, and about 1,208 lines of prose. About 23 per cent of the verse is run-on, and there are 8 light and weak endings. The next longest play is *Richard III* with 3,619 lines, 3,374 of which are blank verse and 170 rhyme, and about 55 lines of prose. About 13 per cent of the verse is run-on, and there are 4 light and weak endings.

The only plays containing no prose are *King John* and *Richard II*. The plays having most prose are *The Merry Wives of Windsor* and *Much Ado about Nothing*. Only one play, *The Winter's Tale*, has no five-foot rhymes in the dialogue proper; the greatest number of rhymes (1,028) is found in *Love's Labour's Lost*, an early play. The highest percentage of run-on lines, light and weak endings is in *Cymbeline*, one of the latest plays. These estimates are only approximate, especially in prose, which varies in extent according to the size of the page.

## A FEW USEFUL BOOKS

### One-volume Editions of Shakespeare

*Shakespeare's Principal Plays.* ed. Brooke, Cunliffe, and MacCracken. Revised edition. 1914. Twenty plays, with introductions, notes, and illustrations.

*Shakespeare.* ed. Hardin Craig. 1931. Twenty-one plays, with introductions and notes.

*The Complete Works of Shakespeare.* ed. Kittredge. 1936. Brief introductions and glossary.

*Shakespeare: Complete Plays and Poems.* ed. Neilson and Hill. New Cambridge edition. 1941. Introductions, notes, and index of characters.

*Shakespeare.* ed. Parrott. 1938. Twenty-three plays, with introductions and notes.

## Editions of Single Plays

Arden, Cambridge, Hudson (revised), Kittredge, Rolfe, Temple, Tudor, Yale.

## Biographies

Adams, J. Q. *A Life of William Shakespeare.* 1923.

Chambers and Williams. *A Short Life of Shakespeare.* 1933. Abridged from Sir Edmund K. Chambers' two-volume *Life.* Reprints valuable contemporary documents.

Spencer, Hazelton. *The Art and Life of William Shakespeare.* 1940. Many pictures. Very readable.

## The Elizabethan Theater

Adams, J. C. *The Globe Playhouse.* 1942.

Chambers, Sir E. K. *The Elizabethan Stage.* 1925. 4 vols. The great authority.

Lawrence, W. J. *The Elizabethan Playhouse.* 1913.

Thorndike, A. H. *Shakespeare's Theater.* 1916. Excellent.

### Shakespeare's England

Harrison, G. B. *England in Shakespeare's Day.* Selections from Elizabethan literature revealing contemporary life.

Raleigh, Sir Walter. *Shakespeare's England.* 1916. 2 vols.

Stephenson, H. T. *Shakespeare's London.* 1905.

Wilson, J. D. *Life in Shakespeare's England.* 1911. Anthology from contemporary sources.

### Elizabethan Literature

Dunn, E. C. *The Literature of Shakespeare's England.* 1936.

Erskine, John. *The Elizabethan Lyric.* 1902.

Odell, G. C. D. *Shakespeare from Betterton to Irving.* 1921. 2 vols. An interesting and very readable book on Shakespearean stage history in England.

Schelling, F. E. *Elizabethan Drama.* 1902. 2 vols.

Seccombe and Allen. *The Age of Shakespeare.* 2 vols.

Wyndham's, Alden's, and Rolfe's editions of Shakespeare's *Sonnets.*

# Index